MORRIS MINOR

THE FIRST 50 YEARS

MORRIS MINOR
THE FIRST 50 YEARS

BY RAY NEWELL

PUBLISHED IN ASSOCIATION WITH THE MORRIS MINOR OWNERS CLUB

Published 1997 by
Bay View Books Ltd
The Red House, 25-26 Bridgeland Street
Bideford, Devon EX39 2PZ

Designed by Bruce Aiken
Edited by James Taylor

ISBN 1 870979 98 2
Printed in Spain

CONTENTS

INTRODUCTION

The Minor will probably be seen as a symbol of British life for many years to come. Here it is on the cover of a 1996 bestseller by American author Bill Bryson.

This publication is a celebration in words and pictures of the first fifty years of the Morris Minor. It seeks to recreate some of the atmosphere of a bygone era when the pace of life was much slower, the price of petrol considerably cheaper and the Morris Minor was an essential part of everyday life. It traces the background to the design and development of the prototype cars, examines the production methods and explores the sales marketing and advertising strategies used. It charts the significant achievements of a remarkable car in endurance testing and motor sport, and considers the various roles the Minor played in the commercial and public life of Britain. It takes an overview of some very unusual Minors and encompasses the very individualistic and specialised interest in customising and modifying. Current interest in the cars and a look to the future conclude a fitting tribute to what many still regard as the World's Supreme Small Car!

The unveiling of the Morris Minor at the Earls Court Motor Show in 1948 was one of the highlights of a prestigious event which helped dispel the austerity of the immediate post-war years. Launched as part of Morris Motors' model range which also embraced the new Oxford and Morris Six, the Minor earned the plaudits for its Tourer and Saloon car versions. Few would have imagined then what the future would hold for this diminutive but

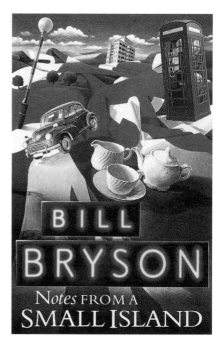

revolutionary design. Even the Morris Motors management could not have predicted the success which would follow, let alone dream of record production levels which would result in a first for the British Motor Industry – a million units for one model and its derivatives – not to mention a production run which would span four decades and end in 1971, in Britain at least.

Alec Issigonis and his small design team could not have anticipated the high regard their prodigy would attain in the eyes of the British public, who took the Minor to their hearts in an unprecedented manner. The car's customers extolled its virtues of reliability, sure-footedness and economy, and ensured through their loyalty a reputation and affection which remains unsurpassed.

The enthusiasm for the Morris Minor was not confined to Britain. Through the efforts of the staff at Nuffield Exports Limited generations of owners all over the world have enjoyed the pleasures of driving their Moggies, Morries and Minors. In so doing, they too have played their part in perpetuating the reputation for British design, engineering and craftsmanship.

Since Minor production stopped, their pleasure has remained undiminished as the car in all its guises has attained cult status. Supported by a thriving network of traders, parts specialists and owners' clubs, the future seems assured as another landmark is reached with the Golden Jubilee of Minor production in 1998.

ACKNOWLEDGEMENTS

This book started to take shape back in 1993, when I proposed it to Charles Herridge and Mark Hughes of Bay View Books. I'm delighted to say that their enthusiasm for the project has remained undimmed and, with their encouragement and the very positive practical help and support of editor James Taylor, justice has been done to the original concept in an innovative way.

Inevitably, putting together information on such a diverse range of topics has meant relying heavily on the personal recollections and acquired knowledge of many people who have been associated with the Morris Minor over the past fifty years. Most of them are referred to directly in the text, but three of them warrant a special mention here. First is fellow Morris Minor enthusiast Russ Smith, currently deputy editor of *Practical Classics* magazine and an acknowledged authority on all things modified or customised; he helped shape the chapters on those topics. Second is Roy Davies, a former employee of Morris Motors Ltd, whose wealth of knowledge about the Cowley works is fully reflected in the section on 'Making the Minor at Home'. And third is Bob Clarke, a KD engineer at Cowley who provided most of the information about exporting the Minor, in consultation with former colleagues including L.P. Coombes, once head of KD Engineering

Sourcing original materials on all aspects of the Minor's fascinating past has also meant relying on the goodwill of many friends and acquaintances, as well as on official sources. Though all photographic contributions have been acknowledged separately (see page 128), I must acknowledge here the invaluable assistance of Morris Minor Owners Club members Keith Fletcher, Phil Marrison, Richard Cownden, Martin Flanders, Sandy Hamilton, Roger Martin, Robin Brown, Lesley Price, Gerry Cambridge and Colin Moles. Once again I find myself indebted to the staff at the Heritage Motor Centre in Gaydon for their help and assistance – in particular to Anders Clausager, Karam Ram and Richard Brotherton. Thanks too must go to Peter Field of the Post Office and to John Colley for the studio photography.

The adoption of this book by the Morris Minor Owners Club as the official publication to mark the Golden Jubilee of the Morris Minor has been an added source of pleasure to me. I am only too happy to acknowledge the help of the current and former editors of the club's magazine, *Minor Matters*, and committee members past and present, and in particular their willingness to permit the use of some photographic materials.

Acknowledgements would not be complete without special thanks to Linda Weselby, who has worked closely with me on the preparation of the manuscript and provided a welcome objective and non-specialist view when it was needed. Of course, thanks also go to my family, who once again have stoically endured the inevitable 'book exile'.

DESIGN AND DEVELOPMENT

The development of what ultimately became the post-war Morris Minor owed more to the specific skills of particular individuals than to the collective foresight or managerial direction at Morris Motors Ltd.

Sir Miles Thomas, whose long association with Morris was rewarded when he was appointed Vice-President of the Nuffield Organisation in 1940, was an influential figure who saw the need for a new range of Morris saloon cars. However, with the war still in its early stages, his immediate priorities included the co-ordination of numerous military projects including the design of armoured cars, tanks and amphibious motor craft. He, more than most, was acutely aware of the talents of a young engineer, Alec Issigonis, who had been recruited from Rootes in 1936 and set to work on the Morris M Ten project. Though Issigonis's inspirational ideas, particularly in relation to independent suspension and rack and pinion steering, had not been incorporated into Morris's first unitary construction vehicle, they were not forgotten. Indeed under the watchful eye of Chief Engineer A.J. Oak, Issigonis's ideas were carefully nurtured.

In his autobiography *Out on a Wing*, Miles Thomas vividly recalled his participation in animated conversations with A.J. Oak and Issigonis while on Fire Watching duties at the Cowley Works, when a 'shy and reserved Issigonis put forward fundamentally new ideas on car construction'. Clearly these ideas made an impact and influenced both Thomas and Oak to give Issigonis a free hand on designing what was to be Morris's new small four-seater car.

Alec Issigonis, later Sir Alec, was born in Turkey in 1907 and died in 1988. The engineer who was the inspiration behind the Morris Minor and the Mini preferred to call himself 'an ironmonger'.

Once government restrictions were lifted in 1943 by the Ministry of Production and major car manufacturers were permitted to return to prototype development, the way was clear for Issigonis to begin work officially on the new project. In anticipation of this permission, a 1/12th scale model of the new small Morris had already been made, and there were numerous sketches from the prolific pencil of the innovative Issigonis. In what is now regarded as a unique situation, Issigonis was provided with a self-contained working area including a small development shop at Cowley. It was here with his long-time assistant, Jack Daniels, and new recruit Reginald Job, that work began in earnest on the new small car.

Daniels, who had previously worked on MGs, had established a successful working relationship with Alec Issigonis during the Morris M Ten Project and continued with various wartime assignments, including the Morris Light Reconnaissance Car which was of unitary construction and had torsion bar front suspension. He also assisted Issigonis with the Gosling, an amphibious motorised barrow, before going on to work on the Tortoise, the largest tank in the world in its day.

Reg Job was a relative newcomer by comparison. Having worked previously at Pressed Steel Company, he joined Morris Motors in 1939. He brought experience of body design to the project and did much to interpret the sketches of Alec Issigonis and produce the technical drawings necessary to have the body panels made. Daniels worked in similar vein with the mechanical specification, bringing to bear his considerable experience of torsion bars, suspension layout and chassis design. In fact he claimed to have 'done the maths behind the suspension' and worked on the floorpan of the new narrow-bodied car which was dubbed the Mosquito. He made no secret of the fact that the suspension layout owed much to his earlier work for MG on the R Type and his pioneering work with the Tortoise tank.

Both men worked well with Issigonis and there was mutual respect. Issigonis rated Daniels as the best all-round draughtsman in the country – high praise indeed. Even in the last month of Issigonis's life in 1988, at a reunion with Reg Job when the author was privileged to be present, the mutual admiration between the two former colleagues was much in evidence. Talk was of Issigonis's sketches and Job's task of interpreting them. Memories drifted back to the Mosquito, coded EX/SX/86, and the first full-size prototype which was built in 1943. Both remembered the small 14-inch wheels, and Alec was quick to point out that they had to have them specially made by Dunlop as none existed at the time.

The Mosquito was perhaps not surprisingly of unitary construction and exhibited many of the features which Issigonis and Daniels had worked on previously, torsion bar suspension and rack and pinion steering being the two most noteworthy. Though the first prototype had been built by March 1943, it was well over a year later – July 1944 – when the first extensive road tests were carried out.

Issigonis was at the wheel when the Mosquito, powered by a Morris 8 Series E engine, made an historic run to North Wales and back. He wrote a report of this journey, which came to light in 1988 when the Miles Thomas papers were discovered. In it, Issigonis reported that the car attracted an almost embarrassing amount of attention, particularly when driving through towns. Feedback from observers was very positive, particularly in relation to the spacious provision for luggage and the interior layout. From a driving perspective, he noted that the suspension was too hard and acknowledged that changes would have to be made – though not on that car as there was restricted suspension movement. He was clearly

agreeably surprised by the comfortable cruising speed of 50-55mph achieved by the side-valve engine and three-speed gearbox, and satisfied with the overall weight distribution. As for the steering, though pleased that the car definitely did not oversteer, he felt that reduction in tyre pressures would eliminate tyre squeal and that directional stability could be improved by some reduction in the front tyre slip angle and with more castor effect.

Overall, this was a positive and rewarding experience which undoubtedly spurred Issigonis on and, with the overall shape of the

Mosquito more or less fixed, he turned his attention to the not inconsiderable matter of the engine. It was always his intention that the Mosquito should have a completely new engine – he had, after all, been given *carte blanche* in its design – and so he set about designing a flat-four power unit. Initial thoughts were that an 800cc version would be available for home market use while an 1100cc version would be used in export models. In the event, this part of the car's development was to prove the most difficult and problematic.

As an interim measure while the flat-four was being developed, an experimental two-stroke engine with two crankshafts and four pistons was tried in the Mosquito. In this unit, one crankshaft was on top of the cylinder block and one below, and the twin pairs of pistons approached and receded from one another. However, it proved to be

Jack Daniels and Reginald Job, Issigonis's capable assistants, were pictured here looking inside the first production Minor, registered NWL 576.

Alec Issigonis was a compulsive sketcher, and in a BBC broadcast to commemorate his 80th birthday he claimed that his drawings were a most effective way of communicating his ideas. In this unique collection of six sketches, sold at auction in 1996 for £25,975, he illustrated the essential features of what would become the Morris Minor. These sketches are reproduced by kind permission of Keith Fletcher.

Signed by Issigonis himself, this fairly late sketch has even later notes proudly claiming that the Minor was 'the first car with 14in wheels and the first car with headlamps built into a transverse front grille.'

This is unmistakably the Morris Minor, albeit in narrow-bodied form. The extension of the front wing shape into the doors was a brand-new idea at the time, inspired by some 1942-season American cars announced in 1941.

The frontal styling was not achieved without a lot of trial and error. Three pages of sketches show the evolution of Issigonis's thinking on the subject.

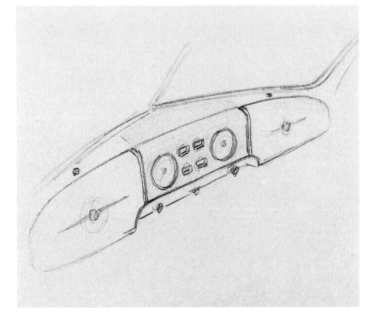

This proposed dash layout for the Minor was actually used at the prototype stage but was subsequently dropped. Aspects of it nevertheless survived in the production models of the Morris Oxford Series MO.

*This very early
narrow-bodied mock-
up of the Mosquito,
with its headlamps
concealed behind the
grille, looks quite
radical for the time.*

something of a curate's egg: above 2500rpm it ran very smoothly, but
below 1000rpm it gave off excessive fumes. It was quickly eliminated
from the programme.

While Miles Thomas tried to ensure that the new flat-four
engine was swiftly developed at the Coventry Engines Branch,
Issigonis went back to the drawing board. In anticipation of a three-
speed gearbox and column gear change, he retained the bench type
front seating and incorporated a folding backrest. Amendments to
the seating resulted in a modification to the roof line which was
raised by three-quarters of an inch. Nor was this to be the last
change, as Issigonis's sketches prompted a variety of front end styling
arrangements. More significantly, though, the width of the car at the
waistline was increased by $1^3/4$in, giving Reg Job a considerable
amount of redrafting to do.

With flat-four engines mated to three-speed gearboxes, tests
began in 1946 in two new prototypes. Though Issigonis himself
favoured the engine, test results in the prototypes were indifferent.
Jack Daniels recalled that while they performed adequately, both the
800cc and 1100cc versions fitted to the Mosquito suffered from
cooling problems. More importantly, they also failed to get the
wholehearted support of management. Issigonis felt that the engine
was 'their version' and not his, and though he kept out of factory

*EX/SX/86, the first prototype Mosquito, was pictured in primer at the Cowley
works during 1943. The louvred bonnet was needed at this stage because the
radiator was positioned behind the engine. Though the outline is remarkably
similar to what was to follow, boot lid design had not yet been determined.*

The column change of the three-speed gearbox prompted the use of a bench front seat. Changes to the seating position led to the height of the windscreen's front edge being raised by 1 1/4 in.

the Mosquito stalled the project for a time, and it was largely due to Sir Miles Thomas's faith that it proceeded at all.

Undeterred, Issigonis and his team pressed on, and further prototypes including a Tourer were built. Proposed launch dates came and went, but by 1947 it was decided that a Morris version of the Mosquito would be announced at the 1948 Motor Show. With the final body shape now determined, preparations for production models were imminent when Issigonis sprang a surprise.

In what is a well documented episode in the development of the Mosquito, he changed the overall width of the car in a momentous eleventh hour decision. In a totally unexpected move he ordered that one of the prototypes be sawn in half lengthways. When he returned the next morning, the two halves were moved apart while he watched. With

Unitary construction was a dominant feature in European car design during the 1940s. This is the floorpan and bulkhead structure of a narrow-bodied prototype. Remarkably, little was changed before the eleventh-hour decision to widen the Mosquito.

politics, the Mosquito project almost fell through. It did not have the full support of Lord Nuffield, who took an instant dislike to the car and referred to it rather disparagingly as a 'poached egg'. Management proposals to introduce MG and Wolseley versions of

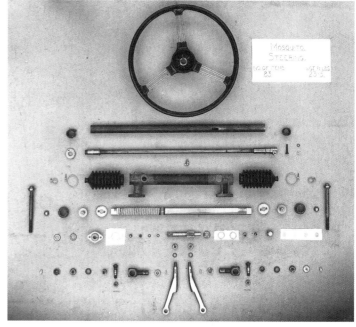

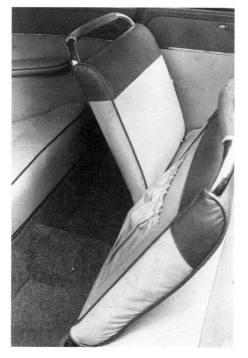

This prototype Tourer, EX/SX/131, was produced in 1947. It shows a further refinement of the front, with a less pronounced vertically slatted grille, and seats with an exposed metal frame.

Some Mosquito features suggested that the 1934 Citroën Traction Avant had influenced Issigonis's thinking. Among them was rack and pinion steering, which was nevertheless innovative in the British motor industry. Component parts of the Mosquito prototype are laid out.

a gap of four inches, the proportions were just right, and Issigonis gave the unenviable task of accommodating the extra width to Reg Job. Reg feared a major rework of the whole body would be necessary, but on reflection he achieved the objective relatively easily and quickly. His solution was to add four inches to the roof and incorporate a raised moulding in the bonnet. In the case of the floor, he added two two-inch strips either side so as to avoid disturbing the transmission tunnel. Unfortunately the bumper blades and valances had already been produced in quantity, and so these were cut in two and a fillet was added.

By this time, roadgoing pre-production prototypes were using a four-speed gearbox with the flat-four engine. However, there were to be a couple of final twists to the pre-production story of the Minor. The first came in November 1947, with the resignation of Sir Miles Thomas, for so long a champion of the Mosquito programme. He

Experimental models featured a number of proposed trim specifications. These two-tone seats with integral storage pocket and functional grab rail were eventually rejected in favour of bucket-type seats on production models.

resigned safe in the knowledge that his recent memorandum dated 14th October would safeguard the new wide-bodied Mosquito and secure its progress to eventual production by 1949. However, this would be at the expense of the flat-four engine, which was to be abandoned in favour of a bored-out version of the existing 918cc Morris 8 side valve.

This move was calculated to bring Lord Nuffield on side, and it worked. In a final memorandum written on the day he resigned, Sir Miles confirmed that the decision had been made to go ahead as rapidly and effectively as possible with the development of the wide two-door Mosquito fitted with the Series E 8hp engine bored-out to 980cc. He also confirmed that the specification would include a four-speed gearbox, central brake and bucket seats. Interestingly, he stated that particular attention should be given to 'an attractive, well tailored' interior.

The scene was set for the final push

towards production. However Lord Nuffield was to have an important last word. In a dramatic turnaround he changed the name of the car insisting that the Mosquito would be called 'The Morris Minor'.

Sir Miles Thomas's successor, Reginald Hanks, oversaw the final stages of development, during which he also approved the Tourer as an additional production model. However, in the meantime, plans to use the bored-out 980cc engine had been dropped, and in February 1948 a mildly reworked version of the Series E 918cc engine was put into the specification.

And so it was that a two-door saloon and a Tourer were prepared for exhibition at the London Motor Show in 1948 as examples of the new Morris Minor. The scene was set for the public to give its verdict on a revolutionary design which had taken six years to get into production.

The new car was finally unveiled at the 1948 Earls Court Motor Show, with the revised designation of 'Morris Minor, Series MM'. For many visitors, it was the outstanding car of the show.

COWLEY EXPERIMENTAL AND THE MINOR

Development of the Minor was carried out by the Experimental Department at Cowley which, like the Drawing Office, was an element of the Morris Motors Engineering Division. It was the Experimental Department which manufactured, tested and approved the prototype vehicles before releasing them to the Production Department. There was, of course, close liaison between the two departments.

The Experimental Department was extensive. Its functions included chassis building, engine testing, body building and trim development. In support of these were a sawmill, an electronics laboratory, a Research and Development department, a Road Proving Department, cold rooms and a 'colonial' test rig. Other rig testing was carried out and the Morris Motors Engineering Department used its export contacts to provide casts of Belgian pavé and of road surfaces from Africa and other areas for the running surfaces at the Motor Industry Research Association proving ground at Nuneaton. It was, of course, the Experimental Department which in 1953 turned a Minor

Traveller into the unique Minor Fire Tender now resident at Gaydon.

The road testers in the Experimental Department used hill courses in the countryside around Princes Risborough and Watlington. Vehicles were subjected to thousands of hill restarts in full road condition and examined at frequent intervals for any deterioration. There was also a 'high-speed' course of 100 miles, which ran from Oxford to Cirencester and back. Vehicles were expected to run to 50,000 miles without trouble – which they usually did. Minors were also taken to West Germany for *autobahn* testing.

The basic durability of the Minor was the reason why the Experimental Department used the car as a 'mule' to develop such things as independent rear suspension, transverse engines and front wheel drive. It was also used extensively for proving the Hydrolastic suspension principle and spent many an hour on Chalgrove Airfield just outside Oxford, famous for its involvement with the Martin Baker aeroplane ejector seat.

DATES AND MODELS AT A GLANCE

Chronology

1943
The Alec Issigonis inspired prototype – the Mosquito – is produced. Features include monocoque body, flat-four engine and independent front suspension.

1948
Late pre-production decisions: prototype widened by 4 inches, giving rise to split bumpers on production cars; uprated Morris Eight Series E 918cc side-valve engine replaced flat-four engine for production models.

1948 (October)
Morris Minor Series MM split-windscreen two-door Saloon and Tourer (convertible) models announced. Minor is promoted as the 'World's Supreme Small Car' and is widely acclaimed at Earls Court Motor Show in London.

1950 (October)
US lighting regulations force a revision of front-end styling. High-headlamp models introduced with the advent of the four-door saloon which initially is limited to export sales only.

1952 (August)
Following the merger of Morris Motors Ltd and Austin Motor Company to form BMC, Austin's 803cc A-Series engine is fitted to some models, later to be designated Series II. Production of side-valve Minors continues in parallel.

1953 (February)
Series MM production ends. Series II models continue in production, fitted with 803cc OHV engine. Only external change from Series MM is a new bonnet motif.

1953 (October)
Traveller model introduced. Commercial range of vans and pick-ups enters production, designated 'Quarter Ton' or 5cwt.

1954 (October)
Re-designed grille with horizontal bars, repositioned sidelights and revised instrument panel with central speedometer.

1956 (October)
Series II range discontinued. New Minor 1000 models announced with 948cc OHV engine, improved front and rearward vision, single-piece windscreen and restyled rear wings.

1961 (January)
Limited edition of 350 Minor 1,000,000 models produced to celebrate production of one million Morris Minors of all types.

1962 (September)
948cc Minor 1000 models are discontinued and replaced by 1098cc Minor 1000.

1963 (October)
Re-designed front and rear light units.

1964 (October)
Modified facia, new style steering wheel, better seating, improved ventilation and heating.

1969 (June)
Convertible models discontinued.

1970 (November)
Saloon models discontinued.

1971 (April)
Traveller, van and pick-up models discontinued.

1949 918cc Series MM Tourer. Low-headlamp models continued in Britain until January 1951.

The Series II models benefitted directly from the Austin and Morris merger to form BMC in 1952, as they acquired the 803cc OHV Austin A-series engine. This one dates from after October 1954, when a new grille was adopted.

The models

1948-53 Series MM

The Series MM Morris Minor two-door Saloon and Tourer models were powered by an uprated version of the 918cc side-valve engine which had been used in the Morris 8 Series E. All Series MM cars had a split windscreen, and the first examples had distinctive low headlamps and split bumpers.

A change in the American lighting regulations forced Nuffield to move the headlamps to the wings with effect from January 1949 for export models and January 1951 for the whole of the range. A four-door Saloon, initially available only for export, was added to the range in 1950 and the Tourer was redesignated Convertible in 1951 when fixed windows replaced the original detachable rear sidescreens. MM production continued until February 1953, by which time 176,002 had been produced.

1952-56 Series II

The Series II cars were introduced in August 1952, and were distinguished by the 803cc OHV A-series engine first seen in the

Right from the outset, the Light Commercial Vehicles or LCVs proved popular with business and commercial users – and Nuffield distributors!

rival Austin A30. Outwardly the only distinguishing sign was a new bonnet motif in place of the Series MM's bonnet flash.

In May 1953, the Quarter Ton commercials (van and pick-up) were added to the range. They shared much of the styling and almost all of the mechanical specifications of the other Series II models, but were built on a separate, all-steel, full-length box-section chassis. The Traveller (estate car) was introduced in October 1953 and used

the same unitary construction basis as the Saloon and Convertible. It featured an ash frame bolted to the steel floorpan, and aluminium roof and side panels.

October 1954 brought changes which included a revised grille and sidelight arrangement (with the earlier honeycomb grille being replaced with horizontal grille bars), a redesigned fascia with central speedometer, and revised interior trim patterns. The Series II remained in production until October 1956, and 318,351 of all types were built.

1956-62 948cc Minor 1000

The Minor 1000 came with an enlarged 948cc OHV engine and much improved gearbox. To this were added a one-piece curved windscreen, a larger rear window and an altered interior.

Leather upholstery gave way to the familiar duo-tone type (used also in the Mini) in the early Sixties. An on-off affair with glove box lids means that early 948cc models have them while 1962 models do not. Semaphore indicators were discontinued in 1961 when flashing indicators were incorporated into the front and rear lamps.

The 948cc Morris 1000 was announced in 1956 sporting a one-piece windscreen.

The Minor Million limited edition cars were essentially 948cc Minor 1000s, with distinctive lilac paintwork, a white leather interior and special Morris 1,000,000 badging. Commercial vehicles, however, continued to follow the general specifications of the model range though with low-compression engines, rubber floor mats and a limited choice of interior colours.

A total of 644,679 948cc Minor 1000s were built.

The versatile estate car was introduced as a 'Traveller's car' in 1953. Along with the commercial vehicles, it remained in production until 1971.

1962-71 1098cc Minor 1000

The last major update was a further increase in engine size to 1098cc, though the cars were still called Minor 1000s. All of them had larger front drum brakes, and from 1963 there were larger rear lights and combination side/indicator lights which allowed for amber flashers for the first time. The 1964 model year brought better seating, a two-spoke safety dished steering wheel and the final variation on glove box lids – an open compartment ahead of the driver and a lidded glove box for the passenger.

The popular convertible continued in production until 1969.

The first Minor to cease production was the Convertible in 1969, followed by the Saloons in 1970. A few later changes such as steering column locks on the last Travellers and commercial vehicles were the only additions before production finally ceased in 1971. Some of the last Minor commercials wore Austin badges and grilles.

A total of 480,825 Minor 1000s were built with the 1098cc engine, bringing the overall Minor production total to 1,619,857.

Although the 1098cc engine was introduced in 1962, the last important revamp of the Minor range was not made until 1964. Note the larger front sidelight/indicator units.

MAKING THE MINOR AT HOME

The first production example of the Minor was a two-door Saloon, built on 20th September 1948 at Morris Motors' Cowley plant, near Oxford. Rave reviews in the motoring press followed the new car's announcement at Britain's first post-war Motor Show a few weeks later, and Nuffield soon found themselves struggling to deal with a considerably greater demand than they had anticipated. A review of production capacity swiftly followed, and within a year, two additional tracks had been put down at Cowley, while a corresponding increase in production capacity at the Engines Branch in Coventry assured an adequate supply of engines and gearboxes.

From then on, production went on increasing, peaking just after the middle of the 1950s and not slowing down until newer designs from BMC stole some of the Minor's traditional market in the subsequent decade. The success of the Minor brought employment and prosperity to Oxford, and helped dispel the post-war gloom in other parts of the country where component manufacturers were kept busy feeding the main assembly lines. In the beginning, the lion's share of production was earmarked for export, but in due course the Minor made its mark – a deep and long-lasting mark – on the life of its native country. This is the story of how those Minors we remember with affection were built.

Assembly of the Minor's bodyshell

British car production in the immediate post-war years differed in many respects to what had gone before, and the emergence of monocoque construction brought to prominence new methods of assembly as well as new processes to prolong the life expectancy of the products.

In the case of the Morris Minor, the components which made up the basic bodyshell were made at Nuffield Metal Products in Birmingham. Huge presses transformed flat sheets of metal into shaped panels which were then placed in specially designed jigs on a moving production line. Phase One concentrated on the assembly of the upper body structure. The majority of the panels were electrically spot-welded, the bare framework being transformed into the recognisable shape of a Minor prior to the point at which, in Phase Two, the complete floor pan unit was welded in.

The completed shell then progressed to the revolutionary

'Roto-dip' rustproofing and roto-spray processes. This consisted of a 500ft long system of innovative baths and sprays which in turn removed grease, provided a rust-proof coating and then applied primer paint which was baked in electrically heated ovens. Two plants had been built at a cost of £500,000 – one for the Minor at Nuffield Metal Products in Birmingham and the second for other Nuffield products at the main assembly plant at Cowley. After passing through the Roto-dip, the Minor bodyshells were taken by lorry to Cowley where the real business of assembly began.

Cowley: incoming supplies

Compared to vehicle production methods at the end of the 20th century, Morris Minor production methods were much more labour-intensive, more physically demanding and much less reliant on sophisticated technology. Though Morris Motors Limited (and BMC after the 1952 merger of Austin and Morris) justifiably claimed the highest production rates in Europe, this achievement

Morris Motors Ltd prided itself on its innovative Roto-dip rust preventative process, which no doubt helped prolong the lives of many Minors. It also explained the presence of a large hole in the back of the battery tray, through which the Roto-dip 'spit' was inserted. Other Morrises went through the Roto-dip – this is a Series MO Oxford.

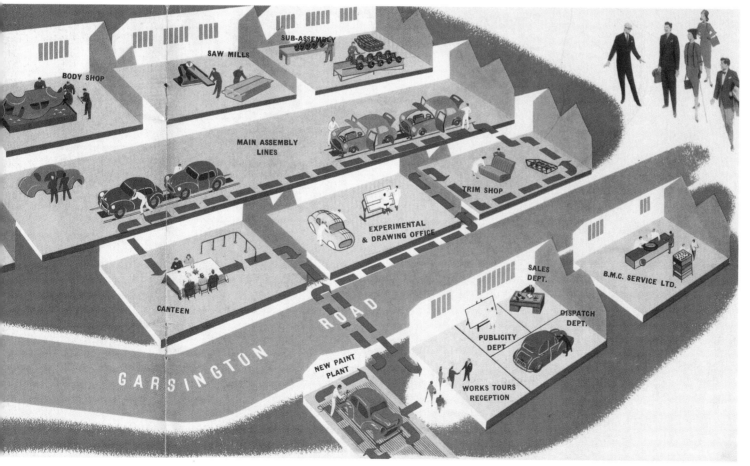

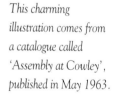

This charming illustration comes from a catalogue called 'Assembly at Cowley', published in May 1963.

This impressive display of the 19,579 parts which went to make one Morris Minor was put on in the Experimental Department at Cowley in 1950.

Burgeoning export orders demanded a constant supply of bodyshells and, as the Minor's popularity increased and home sales resumed, the pressure was on to produce even more in 1951.

masked the huge logistical task required to ensure consistently high standards both in quality control and volume production.

A rare insight into the production methods and working conditions at Cowley has been compiled by former employee Roy Davies, who worked there for over 20 years and was closely associated with Minor production. His account, which follows, is more wide-ranging than anything that the Nuffield Organisation produced for visitors to the plant, and provides a unique behind-the-scenes look at how the Minor was made.

Building the Morris Minor at Cowley was similar to assembling a giant jigsaw puzzle and repeating the process over 30 times an hour, for 44 hours each week. The majority of the components were supplied from outside the factory, either from other Nuffield plants or from approved component and material manufacturers.

Fork lift trucks and palletisation were virtually unheard of in the mid-1950s, and supplies came in a variety of boxes, crates and containers. All of these had to be unloaded and stored manually, while heavier components required the use of hoists.

Suppliers used a great variety of lorries and box vans. Morris

Engines from Coventry used big left-hand drive Mack trucks with chain-driven rear wheels, while Dunlop tyres were delivered in an eight-wheeler box lorry driven by a very large man known as 'Tiny'. He was always on time, and was heartbroken when his lorry was written off in an accident and he was given a replacement 5-tonner truck, which he described as a 'toy'. Lucas used either Foden or ERF lorries, complete with a four-wheel trailer. In order to manoeuvre in the confines of the battery store, each lorry had a coupling at the front so that its trailer could be pushed into the battery bay. Bodies, meanwhile, arrived from the Nuffield Metal Products factory in the Midlands on articulated lorries which usually carried five or six bodies each.

The Body Shop and the Paint Shop

The bodies which arrived from Nuffield Metal Products sported a dark brown primer coat. Those for the Traveller arrived in two separate parts from Coventry Bodies Branch, with the Cab section already painted and the wooden back already assembled and glazed. All the bodies were unloaded by overhead hoists and disappeared into the dark, dank confines of F Block Body Shop. They were then

Care had to be exercised at all times to ensure that no damage occurred to vehicles on the production line – hence the message on the back of the bodyshell here.

lowered onto the storage lines and pushed forward by hand until they reached the motorised conveyor.

The Body Shop always seemed to be cold, even in summer, and in the winter it was particularly unpleasant especially when the bodies arrived wet or – worse still – covered in snow or ice. The bodies were all inspected; damage was corrected by the 'tinnies' (operators using panel-beating tools), and any bodies with heavy Roto-dip paint runs would be held off-line for facing down with emery paper. The operators in the Body Shop also fitted slave equipment to the doors, bonnets and boots, to hold them partially open so that operators in the Paint Shop could spray the interiors.

From the Body Shop, the bodies passed by conveyor into the GK Paint Shop. In contrast to the Body Shop, this was a warm and well-lit environment, heavy with the smell of paint and awash with water on the rubbing decks. The bodies were rubbed down with emery, wiped and sprayed with red paint, and then baked. Following this, they entered the wet rubbing section, where each operator faced off his particular area to achieve a smooth glass-like surface.

Inspectors who were part of the group piecework gang then decided if a body was smooth enough to go forward to the next stage.

They inspected by rubbing a chalk stick at intervals across the surface of the body – and were consequently known as 'chalkies'. If they found a blemish, the offending operator was called up to correct it, thus having to leave his job temporarily. If he could not finish the correction, the line was stopped, and the piecework operators began

Volume production demanded a good stockpile of body parts. Here, wings are stacked ready for transfer to the assembly lines.

Much of the work in the paint shop was labour-intensive, and shells were sprayed with slave supports in place.

This much later picture shows a stock of painted bodyshells reserved for distribution to dealers as replacements for vehicles which had been severely damaged in accidents.

The popular A-series engine block was produced at the Wellingborough Foundry in Northamptonshire. By 1965, one million had been produced – time for a celebration!

to lose money. Culprits were not popular and consequently such occurrences were not frequent!

The painting and rubbing process was repeated through successive coats until the final coats were applied. All painting was completed by hand, with spraying taking place in booths.

From the Paint Shop, the bodies were removed from the trucks on which they had travelled through all the processes and placed on storage lines, ready to begin their journey to the assembly tracks.

M Block: sub-assemblies, paint detail and special equipment for the GPO

While the bodies had been travelling through the Body Shop and the Paint Shop, components were taking shape in other parts of the factory. M Block housed the Sub-Assembly Shop, and here the suspension and associated components were built into recognisable sub-assemblies.

This shop was a low, poorly illuminated building, bitterly cold in winter and very hot in summer. The components themselves were black, cold lumps of steel and the shop layout meant that the feeder store doors were always open. The all-pervading smell in the shop was of the warm oil kept in large tanks beside the assembly area, which had to be kept at a certain temperature so that it could be poured into the steering racks. The smell hung in the air, clinging to clothes, hands and tools. The work here was very heavy with little in the way of mechanical aids.

Rear axles were assembled on a long bench-type construction with V-shaped inverted channel iron sliders. Two operators lifted each axle onto the start of the bench and placed it upside down. The leaf springs – five or seven leaves according to the model – were placed on the axle pads and the U-bolts were then passed through. Rubbers and plates were added, and nuts were run down, usually with a 'windy' (compressed air) drill and socket. Brake pipes and clips were added, and at the end of the bench, each axle was manually rolled over, lifted onto a pair of chains and secured by a wheel nut on each side.

The axle was now on a free-push conveyor rather like a railway siding system, and all hell would be let loose if an axle being fed in caught and tangled with axles running up the main conveyor – a possibility since there were several bench assembly lines. In extreme cases the tangle would cause the conveyor shear pin to break and everything would stop, to the detriment and annoyance of all the operators who were of course on piecework rates.

Steering racks, front suspension units, shock absorbers and other assemblies were fed to the main assembly shop area by means of a Telpher Truck system. These trucks had a central axle and single wheels at the front and rear. They could be used on a floor conveyor with a central pick-up, they could be manually pushed, or they could be lifted by hooks on an overhead Telpher crane.

M Block also housed the Paint Detail Shop. In contrast to the Sub-Assembly Shop this was a warm, comfortable environment with relatively few operatives. They worked at the front of a long U-shaped structure containing the paint booth, oven and cooler. Here, many smaller items for the Minor were sprayed, such as bumper valances, grille panels, grille inserts, door sills, door frames, instrument panel pieces, bonnet mouldings and various components for the commercial derivatives. On completion they were removed, inspected and loaded for onward delivery to the Assembly Shop; most items went into trays or boxes, but valances and grilles were loaded on to 'Christmas Tree' trucks.

A further interesting build area sited next to the warm oven was used for the assembly of the so-called 'freebies' for the General Post Office. These were the specialist components supplied free-of-charge by the GPO for fitting to their red Post Vans and green Engineers' Vans. The 'freebies' consisted of ladders, fire extinguishers, racks, baskets, locks and insignias. Supplies were tightly monitored, and only just enough were supplied for the number of vans in any one contract. There were no spares, so a lost or damaged item was very difficult to replace. In M Block the ladders, racks and racking were assembled and placed on trucks ready for transportation to the Assembly Shop.

J Block (wood) and P Block (trim)

J Block was next to M Block, and here all wooden components were made in what was known as the Saw Mill Shop. This was a dusty but warm shop, where items such as boot boards, seat boards, headlining boards and battery trays were machined. The air was heavy with the smell of freshly cut wood, spirit black and wood preservative. This distinctive aroma came partly from a pressure tank system which was installed to treat headlining boards with a Cuprinol type of liquid and then dry them off with heat. The system had been installed after field engineers had reported complaints of collapsing headlinings from customers in Africa. An investigation had revealed that insects and bugs had been enjoying the taste of the glues in the untreated plywood!

The Trim Shop was always a hive of activity as the predominantly female workforce produced the many and varied items of interior trim.

It was in P Block – the Trim Shop – where seating and other soft components for the vehicle were created. This was the most labour-intensive area of the factory and kept large numbers of women busy on a variety of tasks. Machine operators cut out seat covers, trim and carpets, while others sewed the seat covers in readiness for assembly on long belt conveyors. Small components like door pads, fillets and headliners were glued and stapled, and there was of course a constant smell of glue.

Other sub-assemblies

Several other sub-assemblies also had to be produced and fed to the main Assembly Shop. These included wheels and tyres, instrument panels, and of course the Traveller body.

The Wheel and Tyre Shop produced painted wheels using a dip paint process, and fitted the tyres to these. This was a very arduous process, necessitating ample use of tyre soap, considerable elbow grease and a fair degree of cursing. It became easier with the advent of tubeless tyres, because there were no longer any tubes to nip with the tyre levers! Five wheels were needed for every car produced, and so production rates were very high. The work was also physically demanding, because each wheel and tyre had to be manually moved. Operatives quickly had to learn the art of rolling five tyres side by side to the fitment area in the adjacent Assembly Shop!

Other smaller sub-assemblies including electrical instruments were created in the Panel Room which was staffed by disabled workers, many of them ex-servicemen. In addition, some sub-assemblies were produced at the side of the assembly line itself.

When the Minor Traveller entered production in 1953, a new sub-assembly area called the Body Loft was established. Here, the metal cabs and wooden rear bodies of the Travellers came together for the first time. The Traveller cab came through the paint shop system, but the wooden body arrived separately from Bodies Branch in Coventry, with all its aluminium panels already painted. It was not always an easy task to marry the two together, using a ring of bolts and then sealing the roof join with a heavy rubber gasket. Assembled Traveller bodies were then fed to the Assembly Shop via the Feed Track.

The Feed Track carried the bodies for all varieties of Minor into the Assembly Shop, at the rate of about 60 units per hour. A gap would be created on the track so that the Traveller body could be lowered from the loft to sequence. Few operations were sequenced because of the speed of the Feed Track, but one fascinating exception was the application of the painted coachline. Accuracy was paramount and the operators applied the line with a knife-edged brush. They were able to take a break only when a van or pick-up passed through.

The Assembly Shop

The Assembly Shop contained five assembly lines which passed up the whole length of the shop. Line No.5 was nearest the Feed Track and was used for Saloons and Tourers, while No.1 – which was nearest the main factory entrance – carried the Vans, Pick-ups and Travellers.

A short chassis preparation line was also necessary for the vans and pick-ups because these had a separate chassis. This line ran backwards alongside No.1 assembly line, and was where suspension components were added to the chassis. The chassis of GPO vans

was always finished in aluminium paint, a contract requirement which made it easier to observe cracks in service use.

On No.5 and No.1 assembly lines, the bodies were loaded onto the line standing on 'slave' feet which in turn stood on the twin chain conveyor. This first section of the assembly lines was known as the Erecting Shop and there were pits under all the lines. Some operators worked underneath, while others stood astride the pit with a foot on each conveyor chain. It was not unusual for an operator to find that his trouser turn-ups had been quietly filled with nuts and bolts by his mates working below!

Bodies came down the lines a set distance apart, and this distance was maintained by holding a 12-foot or 15-foot pole between them as they were loaded onto the main conveyor. Production losses cost money to the operatives, who were all on piecework, and so if problems had caused a loss of production, the chargehand would speed the line up by calling for some 'short' loading – that is, the 15-foot gap would be reduced to 12 feet and the 12-foot gap to 10 feet. Sometimes the loaders' enthusiasm was too great, and a shout would go up from the pits that they could not 'see the sky any more'.

The first operations involved lowering the body on to the rear axle and picking up the eyebolt bushes. Then the steering rack, front suspension, exhaust and brake pipes were fitted. Next came the engine, which had been dressed with air cleaner, fan and wiring harness in an area immediately above the Erecting Shop known as the 'Bandstand'. This was also the place where all the assemblies from the Sub-Assembly Shop were stored, and where the Telpher bridge system was located. Brake pipes were formed in the Bandstand, too, starting out as straight Bundy tubing and being shaped over wooden formers. If any assembly problem arose, it was a simple matter to solve it over the lunch hour.

From the Bandstand, engines were lowered through to the assembly line in a carefully managed operation. The Bandstand had a hoist and a dropping area which was three or four vehicles long. Any delay in the process of dropping the engine and gearbox into the vehicle, bolting up and then releasing the hoist bar, could reduce the amount of time the following vehicle had in the engine installation area. If the hoist was still down at the end of the area when the next vehicle was ready to enter, the assembly line had to be stopped.

Once the engine was in, the propshaft was coupled up, together with the exhaust and the designated electrical connections. The

headlinings, windscreens, rear windows, seats and door pads were fitted. Wheels were also fitted as the vehicles passed the Tyre Shop.

Work in the Mounting Shop was much lighter than in the previous shops, and piecework earnings were higher. The operations carried out here involved intricate work which to some appeared to involve almost impossible sleight-of-hand. Windscreens were fitted amazingly quickly with the deft pull of a string here and the stroke of a helper tool there. Operators disappeared into vehicles with a rolled up or a flat headlining to reappear in no time empty-handed and with the lining neatly in place. Specially-designed door pads pushed up against the door, picking up multiple blind fixes. Door handles on the inside were pinned into place under bezels, floor carpets just seemed to flop into place, and seats were fixed in position in the twinkling of an eye. It was all rather special to observe.

With sub-assemblies already completed, final positioning and bolting-up was usually straightforward, if sometimes demanding. Here, rear spring shackle bolts are being fastened.

partly-assembled vehicle then moved on to the end of the pit, which was the domain of the rectification operator who was responsible for finishing any outstanding work. Of course, if he had an unfinished operation which would affect subsequent work he had to stop the track – resulting in more loss of earnings!

After the Erecting Shop, the partly-assembled vehicle moved into the Wiring Shop, where wires, heaters and electrical components were added. It still had no wheels, but was otherwise in a driveable condition – although there was still a lot of work to be done before it would leave the assembly line.

On leaving the Wiring Shop the vehicle then passed under the 'Bridge' and entered the Mounting Shop. The Bridge was a substantial walled structure which enabled operators to pass across all five assembly lines, and contained the offices of the Erecting and Wiring Shops, Supervision, Control Offices and Inspection Offices. It was a commanding structure from which every area of the shops and the Bandstand could be seen.

The name of the Mounting Shop was a relic of the time when bodies were 'mounted' on the separate chassis, and remained in use until the mid-1970s. In the Minor's day, however, it was where

Towards the top end of the Mounting Shop, vehicles arrived at the petrol pumps, radiator fill and battery connection station. Then they would be started for the first time. The familiar sound of the cranked SU petrol pump ticking away as it filled the fuel lines preceded the invariable first-time start, and within minutes another aroma filled the air as paint began to warm on the exhaust pipe.

Vehicles continued on the track which now dipped down before disappearing underground, thus allowing the vehicle's wheels to touch the floor for the first time. The slave stands on which each vehicle had been built fell away and were thrown noisily into a truck for return to the bottom of the track. Each Minor was collected by a driver who then placed it on the Roller Test Rig for its obligatory four minutes' run, when various aspects of its performance would be marked on a card by the tester. From here, completed vehicles progressed under their own power towards the Finishing Line. En route, final adjustments, including wheel alignment and headlamp setting, were carried out.

For Saloons, Travellers, Tourers, Pick-ups and some Vans the build cycle was at an end, though rectification work was

Nearly finished! Headlamp focus and alignment were completed at the end of the track as part of the final checks.

Though road convoys took care of a large proportion of the Nuffield – and later, BMC – distribution, rail dispatch also played its part. Here, complete vehicles are being loaded onto flat-bed railway wagons at the Cowley works.

PRODUCTION LINE HITCHES

The Minor was a good vehicle to build but in the rectification areas there were some aspects which caused a few furrowed brows.

•The front shock absorbers were bolted through into cage nuts in the front beam. With a new operator a cross-threaded bolt was not unknown. The quick remedy was to remove the offending bolt, ask a colleague to lean on the front wing and run a long tap through. However if someone called him and he took his weight off, there was an ominous snapping sound and a lot more work!

•The brake master cylinder was located in the box member below the driver's feet. Access required the removal of some 20 or more bolts which held the combined box member and gearbox cover in place. To seal the cover a rubber gasket was used. The screwdriver had to be kept in place when removing the brass securing screws; if not, they would wind themselves in again as fast as they had been wound out!

occasionally needed. For GPO vehicles, however, there was another stage beyond the end of the Finishing Line. They passed into C Block Tuning Department, where specialised fitments were added. In the early years these included rubber wings, but the bulk of the work always involved the fitting of interior equipment already assembled in M Block. Each GPO vehicle also had an individual road test carried out by a Government Inspector, who was required to write up his findings and sanction whatever action he considered necessary as a result.

The final stop was at S Block, the Dispatch Block. This was where all vehicles were designated for delivery, and items such as tools and literature were added.

Minors built outside Cowley

Although the majority of Morris Minors were built at Cowley, some of the UK production took place at other assembly plants. This mainly involved Traveller models and light commercial vehicles, although 20,000 Minors were built at the MG plant in Abingdon between 1960 and 1964.

Assembly at Abingdon began when the collapse of MG orders

in America brought MG face to face with the prospect of short-time working. Abingdon's General Manager, Cecil Cousins, met his Cowley counterpart, George Walker, for a scheduled Wednesday meeting at the MG plant, and over lunch a deal was struck which took Morris production to the Morris Garages Plant – initially for six months.

MORRIS MINOR PRODUCTION AT ABINGDON, 1960-64

	1960	1961	1962	1963	1964	Total
Traveller	764	1950	2476	4268	1360	10,818
Van		1664	2753	4439	294	9,150
Pick-up			49			49
Total	2428	6389	5278	4562	1360	20,017

Production methods were similar to those at Cowley except that the cars arrived at Abingdon already painted. However, there was one interesting anomaly on the finished vehicles. MG always used to bleed the air from their Armstrong lever-arm dampers to improve efficiency and give the harder ride expected of a sports car. No concession was made to the Morris Minors, whose dampers were also bled with the result that the cars emerged in 'sports car' trim!

The Light Commercial Vehicle Division at Adderley Park, Birmingham also shared a sizeable part of Morris Minor production. Vans and Pick-ups were built there from 1962, and in 1964 all Light Commercial production moved there. When Traveller production was phased out at Cowley in July 1969, this too moved to Adderley Park where it remained until the end in April 1971. Adderley Park also has the distinction of being the last plant in Britain to assemble Morris Minors; in fact, when the last GPO contract was fulfilled in December 1971 and Morris Minor production ended, the Adderley Park plant closed down altogether.

This famous picture dates from November 1970, when the last Morris Minor saloon left the production line. However, all is not as it seems, because this last car was fitted with the wrong engine! After this photograph was taken, the last two cars went straight to the Rectification Department and their engines – one with low compression and the other with high compression – were swapped over. This naturally gave rise to all sorts of quips about not being able to get it right, even after 22 years of trying!

MAKING THE MINOR OVERSEAS

South America may seem an unlikely market for the Morris Minor, but the first example assembled by Automoviles Ingeleses in Mexico is seen here being launched in the customary fashion in 1956.

Overseas assembly was a very important factor in the success of the Morris Minor. Within the Nuffield Organisation – and later BMC – the hub of the overseas assembly operation was the CKD Division at Cowley, which had primary responsibility for the sorting, packing and dispatch of all components necessary for the production of Morris Minors abroad and was initially housed in P Block. The Minor was of course not the only Nuffield or BMC product to pass through the CKD Division, which after 1952 had to deal with Austin as well as Morris models. It nevertheless did account for a large percentage of the total vehicles processed there, particularly during the 1950s.

The CKD Division

In the motor industry, CKD stands for Completely Knocked Down, and is the system where vehicles are shipped abroad in component form, ready for assembly in their country of destination. This method of car assembly became fashionable in the 1940s and assumed greater importance for the Nuffield Organisation as it sought to circumvent the financial constraints and restrictive legislation which governments imposed on the importation of complete vehicles in the wake of World War II. The 'Export or Die' mentality encouraged by the British Government resulted in a major expansion of the original small-scale operation at the Cowley plant, and in the eventual move to a

purpose-built factory with over 100,000 sq.ft. of floor space.

The rationale behind CKD certainly made economic sense. As well as exploiting the potential for vehicle assembly in other countries, it had the added bonus of increasing the capacity for overseas production, especially when UK plants were operating at full stretch. In pure financial terms, it allowed for British vehicles to be assembled abroad while incurring lower tariffs than those attached to fully built imported vehicles. More laudable reasons included opportunities for British expertise to assist in the development of fledgling manufacturing industries in developing markets, the creation of local employment at a time when it was greatly needed, and the chance for locally produced components to be incorporated into the vehicles – once again creating employment and more importantly reducing the amount of foreign exchange spent on imports. A final factor, and one which produced some interesting results, was that CKD assembly allowed local modifications to be incorporated into vehicles in order to meet specific market needs.

The system

In the early days at least, the required build capacity in most CKD markets was very small. As a consequence it was possible to satisfy requirements with the aid of low cost, low technology assembly jigs. In fact, the first Morris Minor jig set consisted of just one fixture in which the complete assembly operation could be performed. As business expanded and new markets were added, the jig design was upgraded and a two-stage facility was developed. With this system, the front end assembly was carried out in a separate fixture and this sub-assembly was then located in the main assembly fixture as the first operation of the main body build.

The checking fixtures used as an aid to quality control supplied to the assemblers were usually standard copies of those used in the UK. However, in some cases fixtures of a simpler design and lower cost were used if the original production equipment was of a sophisticated design. A range of spot welding guns unique to CKD were used, and these were designed to ensure maximum flexibility and minimal congestion in assembly areas.

An indispensable aid to all operatives was the comprehensive manuals supplied by the CKD Division at Cowley. These were heavily illustrated, largely because the assembly operatives in certain countries could not read English, while those in some parts of the world could not read at all!

CKD plants operated in Australia, New Zealand, Indonesia, the Philippines, India, Holland, Denmark and the Republic of Ireland. Small-scale assembly also took place in South America: Automoviles Ingeleses of Mexico started assembling Series II Morris Minors in 1956, though production rates never rivalled those of the Volkswagen Beetle. Bob Clarke, a former CKD engineer at Cowley, recalls that the terms 'knocked down' and 'assembly' were subject to loose interpretation, and suggested that

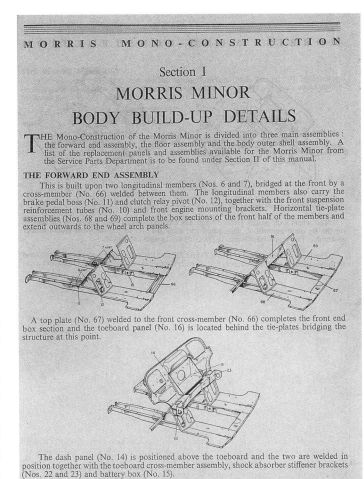

Detailed diagrams like these were vital to overseas operators charged with assembling CKD models.

MORRIS MONO-CONSTRUCTION

Section I

MORRIS MINOR
BODY BUILD-UP DETAILS

THE Mono-Construction of the Morris Minor is divided into three main assemblies: the forward end assembly, the floor assembly and the body outer shell assembly. A list of the replacement panels and assemblies available for the Morris Minor from the Service Parts Department is to be found under Section II of this manual.

THE FORWARD END ASSEMBLY
This is built upon two longitudinal members (Nos. 6 and 7), bridged at the front by a cross-member (No. 66) welded between them. The longitudinal members also carry the brake pedal boss (No. 11) and clutch relay pivot (No. 12), together with the front suspension reinforcement tubes (No. 10) and front engine mounting brackets. Horizontal tie-plate assemblies (Nos. 68 and 69) complete the box sections of the front half of the members and extend outwards to the wheel arch panels.

A top plate (No. 67) welded to the front cross-member (No. 66) completes the front end box section and the toeboard panel (No. 16) is located behind the tie-plates bridging the structure at this point.

The dash panel (No. 14) is positioned above the toeboard and the two are welded in position together with the toeboard cross-member assembly, shock absorber stiffener brackets (Nos. 22 and 23) and battery box (No. 15).

7

Nuffield-approved jigs and checking fixtures were also essential to ensure quality control.

*A new factory was
opened at Amersfoort
in Holland by
Molenaar's during
1953. CKD Minors
continued to be
assembled here until
1966, using a wide
variety of locally-
sourced components.
The Molenaar's
operation was a big
one, supported by an
extensive dealer
network with no fewer
than 52 outlets, and it
supplied vehicles to
other Benelux
countries as well as to
Holland itself.*

for distributors in Mexico and Portugal who assembled Morris
Minors, PKD (Partly Knocked Down) would have been a more
appropriate term. Vehicles were supplied in built-up form but minus
wheels, tyres, batteries and in some cases interior trim, all of which
were supplied by local component manufacturers.

CKD in Ireland

Factory records show that the first CKD Morris Minors dispatched
for export all went to the Republic of Ireland. Eighteen Series
MM Saloons were sent in 1948 to G.A. Brittain in Dublin, an
established company with a long-standing record in car assembly. In
succeeding years Brittain's assembled both versions of the Series
MM, but after the Series II range was introduced in 1953 they
restricted their production to two-door saloons, four-door saloons
and a small number of convertibles. Production ran in parallel with
British plants, and finished in 1971.

   In keeping with the CKD philosophy, Minors assembled in
Ireland exhibited some characteristics which reflected local custom
and practice. Unlike British-built cars, they had their grilles and
road wheels painted in the body colour for all models, while the
wing piping which normally matched the body colour was black on
all Irish cars. On later Morris 1000 models the interior differed
slightly, the most noticeable difference being the plain door trims in

place of fluted heat-formed panels. The real giveaway of the
vehicle's CKD origin, though, was the undisguised evidence of
welding across the bulkhead where the standard one-piece pressing
had been cut in two for packing and transportation.

   The Irish operation was also the source of a most unlikely
difficulty. Teething problems with CKD were not uncommon, but

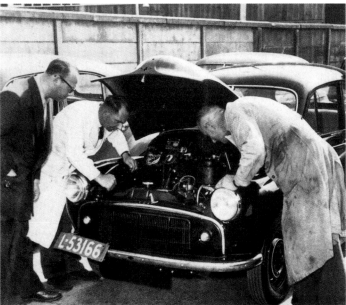

this one was certainly different, as Bob Clarke remembers. He was sent out to Dublin to investigate reported cases of damage in transit.

On arrival, Clarke found that the problem lay in unorthodox unloading methods: the expression 'fell off the back of a lorry' assumed new significance when he discovered that the absence of adequate lifting gear for loads in excess of 1¹/₂ tons meant that the

CKD containers were being tipped off the back of a tipper lorry! The highly skilled operatives did their best to ensure even weight distribution by packing engines at one end, axles at the other, and curved body panels neatly sandwiched between flat ones – but all these efforts counted for nothing as the engines rolled about amongst the vulnerable metal panels. So from then on, additional measures were introduced to secure the contents of the packing cases, and loading and unloading instructions were stencilled on their outsides!

CKD in Holland

CKD was a popular option in Holland. Minor production began there in 1949 with one saloon being assembled in a factory owned by the Molenaar's Company at Jutphaas. As the Minor gained in popularity, production was stepped up and in 1953 a much bigger factory was built at Amersfoort. As in Ireland, only certain models were assembled and the Dutch favoured two-door and four-door Saloons, all of which were built with left-hand drive. Dutch CKD production ended in 1966.

Molenaar's were ideally suited to take on Morris Minor production. They had been producing MGs since 1932, and had added Morris models to their output in 1936. In addition they already had their own established local suppliers of components,

CKD Production Figures – South Africa

Actual volumes by year by model:

Year	2 Door	4 Door	Traveller	Tourer	Total
1950	2215	0	0	0	2215
1951	765	1853	0	0	2618
1952	1638	1140	0	0	2778
1953	1785	1140	0	0	2925
1954	1857	1221	0	0	3078
1955	1920	1124	2 [1]	0	3046
1956	1958	1222	0	0	3180
1957	1594	1469	12	12 [2]	3087
1958	2110	1783	0	0	3893
1959	1111	1137	295	0	2543
1960	964	817	227	0	2008
1961	302	352	156	0	810
1962	324	421	12	0	757
1963	212	177	0	0	389
1964	3	3	0	0	6
Total	18758	13859	704	12	33333
	56.3%	41.6%	2.1%	0.03%	100%

[1] Two prototype Series II Travellers were produced in 1955.

[2] The only twelve convertibles were locally assembled in 1957.

such as Staalglas for windows, Vredestein for tyres, Philips for lighting equipment and Valspar for paint. The provision of such parts helped keep costs down at the point of entry into Holland, a vital consideration because in 1951 no car could be imported into Holland if it cost more than the Dutch equivalent of £420.

Costs were critical and tariffs had to be carefully monitored, as did shipping costs. So Molenaar's worked closely with the Nuffield organisation to ensure that their CKD operation remained viable despite the financial restrictions. One of the benefits of this collaboration was the development of specialised containers which could hold sufficient parts to build six Morris Minors. These were developed by BD Containers for British Rail in conjunction with the Dutch Shipping company HSM Shipping. Once emptied, the containers could be flat-packed for return to the factory; amazingly, they stood a mere 18 inches high when fully collapsed. Their cost

effectiveness helped secure contracts with the high-volume CKD assembly plant at Amersfoort.

CKD in South Africa

South Africa was a latecomer to CKD, preferring to import fully built-up cars up to 1950. As in other markets, the emphasis was on saloon versions, but some Travellers and convertibles were assembled at the plant operated by Motor Assemblies Ltd in Durban. The last Morris Minor rolled off the line there in 1964.

As in the Irish operation, the practice of painting grilles and wheels body colour was prevalent in South Africa. However, the option of standard or deluxe versions, available on fully-built export models, was not incorporated into locally built CKD vehicles. Options such as leather seats and heater were not available either.

CKD in India

Unlike many other BMC products assembled or sold abroad which were marketed under different brand names, the Morris Minor normally retained its identity. Wherever it was made, it was always called a Minor, except in India where the name of Baby Hindusthan was used as a marketing ploy. The name was no doubt inspired by the name Hindusthan given in India to the Minor's big brother, the Morris Oxford Series MO.

Minors were assembled in two different factories in India. Nuffield distributors Addison & Co Ltd in Madras began assembling CKD Morris Minors in 1950 and within a year had produced over 1000. To mark the manufacture of the 1000th Minor, a high-profile exhibition was staged to promote the cars and the highly skilled workforce. Press reports stressed the impressive nature of the displays, which 'showed visitors the process of assembly from first to last'. Starting with the original knock-down shell, they were shown the various stages involving body assembly, engine fitting and the addition of all components necessary to complete the car. Similar processes were undertaken at the Car Assembly Department of the Peninsular Motor Corporation Ltd in Calcutta, where celebrations to mark the 1000th Nuffield vehicle – appropriately a Morris Minor – took place some months later.

CKD in Denmark and Indonesia

The opportunity to take the basic Morris Minor components as part of a CKD package and develop specialised vehicles for specific purposes was within the remit for local assemblers. Few took

LOOK AT IT ANYWAY YOU WANT . . .

It's Big

It's Economical

It's Beautiful

THIS BABY DOES A MAN-SIZE JOB

The Series MO Oxford was sold as the Hindusthan in India, and the Minor was marketed as a 'Baby Hindusthan', perhaps because it was seen as a smaller version of that car.

The new BABY HINDUSTHAN is truly a BIG car built on the same principles and to the same specifications as a big car, and offering you the same luxurious comfort, exciting road performance and attractive features as many a car much costlier to buy and maintain.

The BABY HINDUSTHAN'S high-efficiency Over-Head Valve engine squeezes every bit of power out of every drop of fuel! Torsion bar independent front suspension, double-acting shock absorbers front and rear, and within-the-wheelbase seating ensuring maximum riding comfort. Four-speed synchromesh gear-box, hypoid final drive and four-wheel fully compensated hydraulic brakes ensure safer and effortless driving.

The interior of the BABY HINDUSTHAN is tastefully finished, with spacious accommodation for four, and room enough for an occasional fifth. The luggage booth has 7 cubic feet of usable space.

In short, when you buy the new BABY HINDUSTHAN, you can be sure that you are getting the finest kind of economical motoring. No other car returns so much satisfaction per mile for so little cost!

advantage of this option, preferring to build cars to the original basic specification. But exceptions included CKD assemblers in Denmark and Indonesia who offered their customers something different from standard production models.

The Danish offering – produced by DOMI (Dansk Oversoisk Motor Industrie), a well established company – was a revised version of the Morris Minor Van. Produced in both Series II and 1000 versions and built on a standard chassis, it had increased capacity by virtue of a longer body, a virtually flat roof which was integral with the cab, a single opening rear door with a one-piece window and newly designed side panels. Interior trim specification was to local standards and additional fitments included a latticed partition behind the driver.

In Djakarta, Indonesia, variations on this theme were produced by P T Java Motors Ltd. Again using a standard Morris Minor chassis and cab, a 'people carrying' vehicle was produced. Cowley's Bob Clarke recalls that early versions of these unique Morris Minors were constructed by adding ordinary pick-up sides and the aluminium roof from the Traveller models, the roof being supported by locally-made helical brass fitments. Transporting the aluminium panels proved difficult, and perhaps due to the heat and humidity later versions adopted wooden roof structures which had open spaces for windows to allow for ventilation!

Certainly later versions dispensed with the original style of factory-produced pick-up sides, favouring instead home-made

versions. Local content for what are arguably the most unusual buses or taxis you are likely to see was very high, with the whole of the rear section and seats, wheels and tyres being locally sourced.

CKD in the Philippines, Australia and New Zealand

In contrast to these unusual Minors, more conventional vehicles were produced in the Philippines, where the Mascott Trading

Morris Minors proved a popular choice in India, and assembly at the Peninsular Motor Corporation in Calcutta reached a significant landmark in 1951.

Company assembled saloon and tourer models. However, the largest assembly plants for Morris Minors outside the UK were based in Australia and New Zealand.

In Australia many of the early models were imported as complete vehicles. However, once assembly of CKD Minors began at Nuffield (Australia) Pty Ltd in Zetland, New South Wales, production rates climbed steadily, so much so that the company was able to exert pressure on the Nuffield Organisation in the UK and agree the use of locally designed jig assemblies for body construction. Local content was high in the Australian models. Paint types and colours were indigenous and, unusually on CKD models, engine, gearbox and back axle components were sourced from the Nuffield-backed engine plant in Sydney.

Two Morris Minor offerings from DOMI in Denmark. Features of the van include a longer body, a single rear door and redesigned side panels.

DE FÅR MEST FOR PENGENE I EN

MORRIS 1000 SUPER STATIONCAR ELLER COMBI

Locally designed and adapted to suit local climatic conditions, these Indonesian Morris Minor 'people carriers' plied their trade in Djakarta.

Overseas distributors marketed a variety of special-edition Minors. This Tourer, complete with a fully-retractable hood, was produced by Malayan Motors of Singapore.

Australia was the Minor's largest overseas market. The large factory built near the racecourse in Sydney assembled Minors from CKD kits, although in the early years many cars had been imported in fully-built condition. The fleet of 30 locally-assembled Minors pictured here was supplied to the Metropolitan Water, Sewerage and Drainage Board.

New Zealand also boasted a thriving assembly plant at Dominion Motors Ltd in Auckland. Built in 1939, the impressive factory employed 600 people in 1952. Like Australia, New Zealand imported fully-built cars as well, but restricted quotas increasingly encouraged local production using CKD kits. Some components were sourced locally, the main ones being soft trim items, carpets, glass and wiring harnesses, as well as wheels, tyres and batteries. As in some other territories, engines in the New Zealand-built cars did not always change at the same time as those in the UK-built models. Consequently, the 948cc engine is more likely to be found in New Zealand-built Morris Minor 1000 models than the later 1098cc version.

The Dominion Motor Plant has the unusual distinction of being the last plant in the world to manufacture Morris Minors. Production continued until 1974, by which time 1.6 million units had been made world-wide.

SELLING THE MINOR

When the Minor was first announced in 1948, sales and promotional material covered the complete new Morris range, which of course embraced the MO-Series Oxford and MS-Series Six as well as the Minor itself. However, when attention eventually focused exclusively on the Minor, certain predictable themes emerged, and in succeeding years these were exploited to the full. Inevitably the Minor's size came in for special scrutiny and much was made of what the copywriters called its 'Big Car Features'. Economy, performance and comfort were additional selling points but it was the notion of a quality product with worldwide appeal which dominated the early sales brochures and advertising literature.

The concept of the Global Market was much in vogue, particularly when the Series MM models entered production, and almost all advertising literature reflected this quite overtly. However the eleventh-hour decision to abandon the narrow-bodied prototype and widen the Minor by four inches must have given the advertising designers nightmares. While the production engineers got on with the job of producing the revamped body, the ad men stuck with the pictures they already had, and consequently some of the early promotional material is more indicative of the prototype cars than of the real production specification!

Surprisingly, early American brochures did not contain illustrations of LHD cars. Instead, RHD versions were illustrated, and an overprinted note advised that LHD versions were available for the American market. American terminology was used though, and Minors became sedans instead of saloons, ran on gasoline instead of petrol, and acquired a hood instead of a bonnet and a trunk instead of boot. In addition, some evocative descriptions were included. The Minor's rear-hinged bonnet was described as an 'alligator hood' while the term 'lullabye ride' was used to describe the comfort of its suspension!

By the time Series II models were introduced after the BMC merger, the emphasis had changed slightly. Quality was now the watchword, and 'Quality First' was the way the copywriters put across their message about Morris products. The Minor by now had a proven record for performance, economy and practicality, and so these qualities were also used in its promotion. The house style

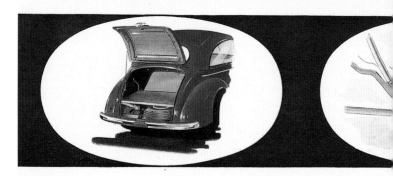

★ "A small car interpretation of a big car specification." *That describes the new Morris Minor.* No other small car anywhere in the world has so many big car features as the Morris Minor. Independent torsion bar front suspension .... "Monoconstruction" of body and chassis .... all passengers seated within the wheelbase .... these are but a few of the features which make the **MORRIS MINOR** *the world's most advanced, most wanted small car.*

★ "Monoconstruction"—the technique of combining body and chassis in one all-steel safety structure, achieving immense strength with valuable saving in weight.

★ Inter-axle seating for maximum comfort and freedom from "dip and sway."

★ Safety doors, hinged at forward edges, with private lock to driver's door and safety catch to passengers' door. Wide opening for easy entrance and exit.

★ Hypoid bevel gears to rear axle assembly for long silent life, and high ground clearance.

★ Internal bonnet lock, operated from driving seat, with ingenious safety catch in radiator motif.

The NEW **MORRIS** MINOR

The World's Supreme Small Car

★ *Designed on Big Car Lines —*

THEN SCALED DOWN TO MAKE IT THE MOST ECONOMICAL

Real Car — EVER TO BE BUILT ANYWHERE IN THE WORLD

The world-wide appeal of the 'new Morris Minor' was a selling point right from the outset, as two images from this 1948 brochure show. Designed on big car lines with big car features, the 'World's Supreme Small Car' had much to offer, including 'economical motoring' – a big consideration just after the war.

All told, the Morris Minor had a great deal to offer in terms of innovative design, passenger comfort and safety, as well as a whole new range of colourful exterior paint finishes.

...ar in the world that embodies all these **BIG CAR FEATURES**

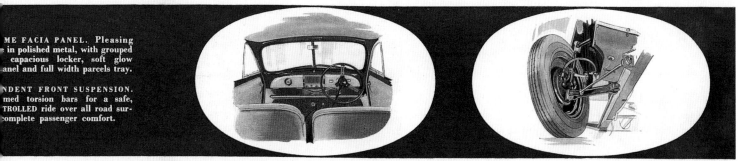

...ME FACIA PANEL. Pleasing ...in polished metal, with grouped ...capacious locker, soft glow ...anel and full width parcels tray.

...NDENT FRONT SUSPENSION. ...med torsion bars for a safe, ...TROLLED ride over all road sur-...complete passenger comfort.

★ LARGE LUGGAGE BOOT. Seven cubic feet of space for all passengers' luggage, plus extended floor when rear seat squab is dropped. Access by hinged exterior trunk lid, or from interior by hinged back seat squab.

★ SURE, SAFE BRAKING. Time-tested Lockheed hydraulic, with double leading-edge shoes on front for responsive, balanced, SAFE braking in all emergencies on all surfaces at all speeds.

★ "Alligator" bonnet giving exceptionally easy access to engine and auxiliary equipment.

★ Handsome low frontal appearance on "big car" lines to lessen wind drag.

★ Hinged safety glass panels on leading edge of door windows for controlled ventilation.

★ Latest pattern long-wear safety-tread Dunlop tyres and tubes.

★ Double-acting Luvax type hydraulic shock absorbers front and rear.

★ Concealed trafficators with hand switch and warning light conveniently mounted.

★ Separate front bucket seats with hinged backs and one-movement adjustment for height as well as fore and aft positioning.

★ Choice of saloon or convertible body styles. Convertible has easily erected fully weatherproofed equipment and winding glass windows to doors.

★ Choice of three colour styles—Romain Green, Platinum Grey, or Black. Wings and body finished same colour. Interior trim in tasteful neutral shades.

changed little, but with the advent of the Morris 1000 came a new emphasis. This time, it was the idea of the car's versatility and its broad appeal to both men and women which prompted a change of tack and the emergence of a new theme, 'Together you'll choose'. The importance of overseas sales rose once again, and although overseas sales material invariably used the same artwork as its home equivalent and put across essentially the same message, the brochures retained a distinctiveness which now makes them quite collectable.

Advertising of a different kind was used to good effect in the motoring press and trade journals. In what is best described as opportunist advertising, much was made of significant landmark events in the development of the Minor. Classic examples include the highly publicised 10,000 miles non-stop run in 1952 (see page 80), which prompted everybody who had anything to do with the supply or manufacture of parts for the Minor to advertise in important journals such as *The Autocar*.

When the Morris Minor became the first British car to reach the magical figure of one million units manufactured in 1961, a unique marketing opportunity presented itself and of course BMC seized it. In subsequent years, even though more modern designs such as the Mini and the front-wheel drive 1100 range made clear that the Minor was a relatively old design, publicity material made much of the fact that millions of owners could attest to the virtues of the ubiquitous Morris Minor.

Support for traders was also provided through block adverts and these were used extensively in local newspapers and magazines. They encapsulated the essential character of the Minor in all its guises – albeit with the assistance of a little artistic licence, as the accompanying illustrations show!

'Quality First' became a dominant marketing theme for Morris vehicles in the mid-1950s. It was used extensively on in-house advertising literature and featured prominently in contemporary motoring magazines, including this 1954 front cover.

The Autocar, 7 May 195

THOUSANDS OF
MILLIONS
of road miles prove it

The "quality first"
MORRIS MINOR
is still the world's biggest small car buy!

What does this mean to you? Just this: that when you buy a Morris Minor you know, beyond doubt, that your money is wisely spent. In advance of you, thousands of motorists—millions of actual road-miles—have *proved* that this is indeed 'the world's biggest small car buy'.

Remember too: 'big' means more than 'size' in the Morris Minor. It means—in feature upon feature, in economy and long-term service—that EXTRA quality and value that Morris have always given to the motorist. Yes—you'll be glad you bought a Morris Minor!

SERVICE IN EUROPE:
Qualified Morris owners planning a Continental Tour are invited to see their Morris dealer for details of a free service to save foreign currency.

MORRIS MINOR · OXFORD · SIX — Fitted with Safety Glass throughout

MORRIS MOTORS LIMITED, COWLEY, OXFORD.
London Distributors: Morris House, Berkeley Square, W.1. Overseas Business: Nuffield Exports Ltd., Oxford, & 41 Piccadilly, London, W.1

C.C. 97

8 AUGUST 1958

1/-

The Autocar
FOUNDED 1895   LARGEST CIRCULATION

"0-60 in 28 secs—
it's the small car
with big ideas"

"Will take us all in comfort—
it's the small car
with big
proportions"

Together you'll choose a

"QUALITY FIRST"

MORRIS
MINOR 1000

Morris owners planning a Continental Tour are invited to see their Morris Dealer for details of a free service to save foreign currency.

TWELVE MONTHS' WARRANTY—Backed by B.M.C. Service, the most comprehensive in Europe.

PRICES FROM £415 (Plus £209 . 7 . 0 Purchase Tax)

MORRIS MOTORS LIMITED, COWLEY, OXFORD.
London Distributors: Morris House, Berkeley Square, W.1. Overseas Business: Nuffield Exports Ltd., Oxford, and at 41-46 Piccadilly, London W.1

The increasing popularity and proven reliability of the Morris Minor undoubtedly helped perpetuate its reputation as a good buy. Few owners would have quibbled with the claims made in this May 1954 advertisement for The Autocar.

With the advent of the Minor 1000 range, a new theme – 'Together you'll choose …' – emerged. Increasingly, advertising reflected the attraction of the Morris Minor for women drivers, as in this 1958 front cover of The Autocar.

It takes us out for weekend spins!

When you buy a family car you consider not only economy, performance and comfort but your safety and that of your passengers — your family. Every improvement in the new Morris Minor 1000 has this end in view — the increased visibility, of the one-piece windshield, the new deep-sunk centre steering wheel, the bigger, more agile overhead-valve engine, and the improved general performance and acceleration that it brings.

The roadholding of the Minor 1000 is unquestionably superb and the increased power makes it even more delightful to drive. You will be proud of your Morris Minor — for its handsome speedy lines, for its gay colours and tasteful hardwearing interior upholstery — for its irrefutable operating economy.

No other car returns so much satisfaction per mile for so little cost! No other car gives such generous value for money. Now, more than ever, it is " The world's biggest small car buy ".

The appeal of the Morris Minor as a practical family car shines through in this 1956 brochure, which promoted the new and improved Morris 1000 model range.

Togetherness again, once more on the cover of The Autocar but this time during August 1960.

It was inevitable that the Minor's record-breaking production run of one million vehicles by December 1960 would be reflected in BMC's advertising and sales literature. This spread (right) is taken from a 1961 sales catalogue for the Minor 1000.

AUSTIN
6 cwt/8 cwt van & pick-up

Chosen by more than a million motorists all over the world

No other car from Britain has had so successful a run as the Morris Minor. And still it goes from success to success. Its performance is brilliant—limpet-like road-holding, hair's-breadth steering accuracy, gone-with-the-wind acceleration! Above all, economy. Think of driving 40-odd miles and having to buy only one gallon of petrol.

The Morris Minor 1000 proves to many a woman that she's an excellent driver. She can slip in and out of tight parking spaces and dart light-heartedly through town traffic with ease. How nice to think that the car he wanted was just the car she wanted him to want.

First British car to pass the million
'QUALITY FIRST' MORRIS MINOR 1000

MINOR 1000 4-DOOR SALOON

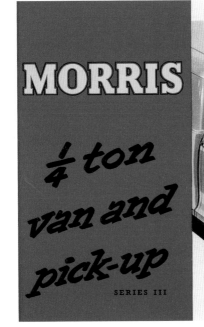

MORRIS
¼ ton van and pick-up
SERIES III

MORRIS *Minor* 2-DOOR SALOON

"Quality First"—all the way through

Advertising literature for the Light Commercial Vehicles concentrated on the practical and functional nature of the van and pick-up models. Colourful and visually appealing, the brochures effectively demonstrated the potential that those vehicles had for commercial and business enterprises. In later years, the Minor LCVs were also available with Austin badges. Promotional postcards (above) for the Series II Morris Minor two-door saloon emphasised the 'Quality First' theme, and are now quite collectable.

Colour 6   MOTOR week ending October 24 1964

CHOOSE MORRIS
THE SUCCESSFUL CARS

Nothing succeeds like choosing success! Morris success is a built-in guarantee of motoring satisfaction. It means that every car is designed, engineered and priced right. Use it as your yardstick at the Show. If so many more motorists find the best answer in a Morris – and they do – isn't it likely that you will too?

Mini-Minor Most spectacular success in motoring history! Mini, Mini Super de-luxe, Mini-Cooper and Mini-Cooper 'S' now with Hydrolastic® suspension. Mini-Traveller.

Minor 1000 Britain's most highly-proved car – with over 1,250,000 enthusiastic owners. Minor 1000 Saloon (2 and 4-door) Convertible and Travellers.

Morris 1100 The brilliantly-engineered Morris 1100 is acclaimed all over the world as one of the most advanced cars ever produced.

Oxford Motoring's most successful combination of power, space and luxury – at a reasonable price! – Saloon and Traveller. Automatic transmission available.

All Morris models are warranted for twelve months and backed by B.M.C. Service.

MORRIS MOTORS LIMITED, (SALES DIVISION) LONGBRIDGE, BIRMINGHAM • OVERSEAS BUSINESS: NUFFIELD EXPORTS LIMITED, OXFORD AND AT 41-46 PICCADILLY, LONDON, W.1

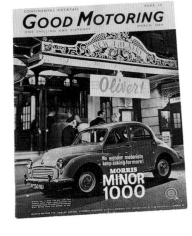

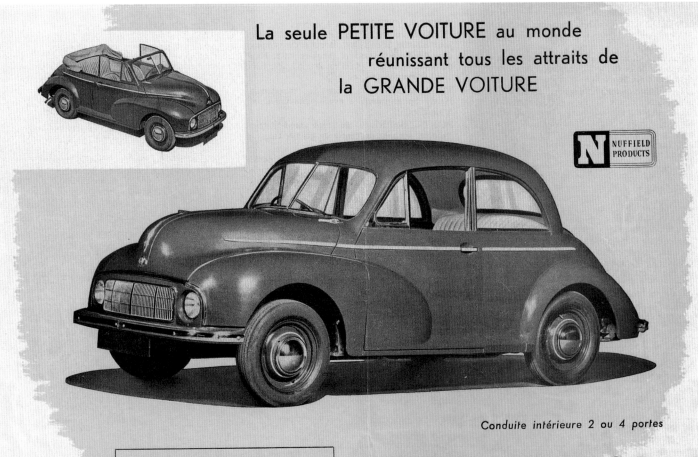

La seule PETITE VOITURE au monde
réunissant tous les attraits de
la GRANDE VOITURE

NUFFIELD PRODUCTS

Conduite intérieure 2 ou 4 portes

LA NOUVELLE MORRIS MINOR

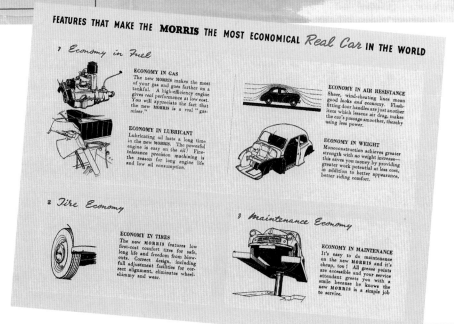

FEATURES THAT MAKE THE **MORRIS** THE MOST ECONOMICAL *Real Car* IN THE WORLD

1 Economy in Fuel

ECONOMY IN GAS
The new MORRIS makes the most of your gas and goes farther on a tankful. A high-efficiency engine gives real performance at low cost. You will appreciate the fact that the new MORRIS is a real "gas-miser."

ECONOMY IN LUBRICANT
Lubricating oil lasts a long time in the new MORRIS. The powerful engine is easy on the oil! Fine-tolerance precision machining is the reason for long engine life and low oil consumption.

ECONOMY IN AIR RESISTANCE
Sheer, wind-cheating lines mean good looks and economy. Flush-fitting door handles are just another item which lessens air drag, makes the car's passage smoother, thereby using less power.

ECONOMY IN WEIGHT
Monoconstruction achieves greater strength with no weight increase—this saves you money by providing greater work potential at less cost, in addition to better appearance, better riding comfort.

2 Tire Economy

ECONOMY IN TIRES
The new MORRIS features low first-cost comfort tires for safe, long life and freedom from blow-outs. Correct design, including full adjustment facilities for cor-rect alignment, eliminates wheel-shimmy and wear.

3 Maintenance Economy

ECONOMY IN MAINTENANCE
It's easy to do maintenance on the new MORRIS and it's cheap, too! All grease points are accessible and your service attendant greets you with a smile because he knows the new MORRIS is a simple job to service.

The advertising department were at least consistent in their marketing of the Minor, whatever language was used.

Towards the end of production, the Morris Minor was pushed into the background as new models came to prominence, a fact reinforced by this 1970 British Leyland advertisement (far left). Innovative ideas were used to good effect in motoring journals, and 1964 covers from Good Motoring (upper left) illustrate the point well with reference to the popular musical Oliver and a 'case proven' verdict. The universal acclaim with which the Morris Minor was received is well illustrated (lower left) in this advertisement, which has a truly international flavour.

Although America was an important overseas market, early brochures used pictures of British-market cars, overprinted to reassure potential owners that their cars would be supplied with left-hand drive! By the time of this 1951 brochure, the illustrations reflected what the left-hand drive car really looked like – and used American motoring terms and spelling as well.

Crating up cars for a variety of overseas destinations was a labour-intensive process. Such was the demand for Nuffield products that new facilities had to be built at Cowley in the 1950s.

Forenade Bil were the Nuffield distributors in Malmo, Sweden. They were valued customers whose volume sales prompted this commemorative photograph of the 20,000th Nuffield vehicle to be shipped to them in the post-war period.

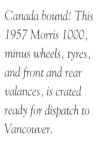

Canada bound! This 1957 Morris 1000, minus wheels, tyres, and front and rear valances, is crated ready for dispatch to Vancouver.

Overseas: Nuffield Exports

Nuffield Exports was a thriving part of the Nuffield organisation in the 1950s. Great emphasis was placed on securing new markets throughout the world and, as the number of distributors mushroomed, representatives from the Nuffield organisation – including Lord Nuffield himself – toured the world glad-handing company representatives, Government Ministers and local officials. Meanwhile, Cowley played host almost daily to trade delegations and overseas distributors as well as to engineers and technicians. The effort of all concerned paid handsome dividends in terms of increased employment, sales and staff morale. By 1955, as exports of the Morris Minor approached an all-time high, the list of distributors read like a world gazetteer and reached well beyond the far-flung corners of the British Empire.

Sir Leonard Lord, Chairman of the British Motor Corporation, announced in 1955 that the Corporation had that year exported more vehicles than any other motor manufacturer in the world: nearly 200,000 vehicles, with a total value of approximately £75 million. During 1955, nearly four vehicles were produced every minute of the working day, in spite of industrial disputes which affected some of the supplying companies. The total output for the year, which constituted a record for the British Motor Corporation (and for all other British companies), was 468,943 vehicles. As Lord pointed out, no other motor manufacturer outside America had ever achieved this level of output, and even in America it had only been exceeded by three of the great corporations there.

Teams of convoy drivers ensured that vehicles adhered to the tight delivery schedules by driving them directly to the docks. Here, Morris Minors, Oxfords and Sixes await embarkation on the Bencleuch, en route to Singapore.

J.S. Inskip was the Nuffield distributor on the East Coast of the USA. These high-headlamp Series MM Tourers were the first to reach Inskip's, in 1949. High headlamps were introduced to meet US lighting regulations; at this stage, cars for the rest of the world still had the original low-light design.

Overseas trade fairs provided additional opportunities to promote Nuffield products. This display put on by DATIM, the distributor in Morocco, used advertising and promotional materials to good effect.

Victor Hills was Lord Nuffield's chauffeur on the occasion of his visit to Ceylon in 1947. He also personally supervised the unloading of this car, the first Morris Minor in Ceylon, and drove it from the docks to the British Car Company's new premises. Lord Nuffield travelled widely to promote Nuffield products and to encourage the establishment of dealer networks. His support of this new venture – Oxford House in Ceylon – is evident from this personal letter and was typical of his willingness to encourage an entrepreneurial spirit.

It is important not to lose sight of what was behind this achievement, and to recognise that it had been made possible by careful co-ordination of the work of hundreds of BMC employees. These ranged from the pool of 100 convoy drivers who delivered vehicles to the docks on a daily schedule, through the employees responsible for loading vehicles on to the flatbed railway wagons at each of the five sidings at Cowley, to the dispatch clerks whose task was to ensure that all the paperwork, permits and export licences were in order.

Such was the volume of trade that ships were chartered specifically to meet demand. Sizeable cargos were commonplace: examples are the delivery to Australia of 1636 Nuffield vehicles by the *SS Lausanne*, and the delivery to Dominion Motors in New Zealand of 379 cars aboard the *SS Rippington Grange* – a cargo which took three days to unload.

Even at the port of entry the job was often not complete. In some territories, particularly in Africa and South America, the road infrastructure was so poor that vehicles had to be air-freighted to the point of distribution. This was the case in Colombia, for example, where the road route to the capital of Bogota was so poor that vehicles had to be flown from the port of arrival at Barranquilla, on the Caribbean.

THE NUFFIELD
ORGANIZATION
COWLEY OXFORD

For over twenty years, the British Car Company has held the franchise for Morris Cars in Ceylon, and, during those years, their enthusiasm, loyalty and business acumen has never faltered. It gave me the greatest pleasure, during my brief visit to Colombo last year, to once again meet Mr. W.C. Wishart and many of the Executives and Staff, and to see the extensions to the buildings then under construction. In particular, I was impressed with the general efficiency and the undoubted happy relations which existed there.

I am certain the bond which has been created over the years between my Organization, and the British Car Company, will increase in the future.

I therefore take this opportunity of wishing success and happiness to everyone concerned with the enterprise.

3rd December, 1948.

Excitement would be high at an overseas distributor when a consignment of new vehicles arrived from England. At Rowlands Ltd in Ceylon, Victor Hills was responsible for supervising the unloading of the first Morris Minor dispatched to Colombo. He had to devise a suitable method of ensuring safe transfer of the cargo to the dockside, and still vividly remembers his drive back to the garage. It was the culmination of a lot of hard work following Lord Nuffield's visit to the company in 1947, when Victor had acted as his chauffeur. Most importantly, it signalled expansion for what became the British Car Co. Ltd. This scenario was re-enacted throughout the world, and it made a significant contribution to the story of the vehicle which Nuffield's copywriters had from the beginning called the 'World's Supreme Small Car'.

This rare left-hand drive split-windscreen Traveller was photographed in 1996 in Portugal, where it was first registered. After years of service as a garage runabout, it has been fully restored by José Alberto Gama Ribeiro, the son of its original owner.

As its number-plate suggests, this restored left-hand drive Traveller is still in use – in California – as a company car for Ideas Inc and its proprietor.

OWNING AND DRIVING THE MINOR

Those were the days: a 1951 Minor four-door saloon passes the pumps of a filling station complete with the obligatory Redex dispenser, somewhere in rural England.

All the euphoria and advertising hype surrounding the launch of the new Morris Minor inevitably raised expectations in 1948, and prospective British owners flocked to their local dealers. Sadly, many of them had their hopes of driving their own Morris Minor cruelly dashed. In fact, you stood a better chance of acquiring a new car if you lived in Melbourne or Sydney than if you lived in London or Oxford. There were two reasons for this: one was a shortage of new cars for sale in Britain at a time when the vast majority were being built for export, and the

other was the Covenant Scheme which governed the purchase of a new car in the immediate post-war era.

The Covenant Scheme was introduced in 1946 by the British Motor Trade Association, and was intended to hinder the development of a black market in new cars at a time when these were in short supply in the immediate post-war years. Under the scheme, customers had to sign a covenant agreeing not to sell the vehicle for two years and agreeing that no-one else would be permitted to use it.

The Covenant Scheme was open to all kinds of abuses, but it was still in operation in 1952 when the then Secretary to the Association, K. C. Johnson Davies, explained: "The demand for cars is of such magnitude and the permitted allocation to the home market so small that nine out of ten waiting customers are bound to be disappointed. Nothing can remedy that situation except the release of more cars to the home market; the necessity, in the interests of the country's economy, to export 75% of our total production remains and will continue to be a grim reality. All that can be done, is being done, in the face of unbelievable difficulties by the motor trade, to ensure that those who do receive the few new cars that are available have a genuine and essential need of a car for their own use; that they have not previously had one or more post-war cars; and that they get these cars at their proper price as fixed by the manufacturers, plus Purchase Tax".

The premises of P. Pierce, who ran the Ercall Garage in Shropshire, present a picture of the typical Nuffield agent in the English countryside during the 1950s and early 1960s. Through that door in the centre was the spares counter, manned by a helpful, knowledgeable, white-coated member of staff, and through the door on the left was the workshop, with Minors in evidence among the other vehicles in for repair or maintenance.

BRITISH PRICES (INCLUDING TAX)

Series MM			
1948	£358	10s 7d	Saloon and Tourer
1950	£382	6s 11p	Tourer
1951	£585	12s 3d	Four-door Saloon
Series II			
1952	£631	10s 0d	Four-door Saloon
1953	£599	13s 4d	Basic Traveller
	£622	6s 8d	Deluxe Traveller
1954	£529	10s 0d	Four-door Saloon
1955	£622	6s 8d	Traveller
Minor 1000 (948cc)			
1956	£668	17s 0d	Four-door Saloon
1958	£734	2s 0d	Traveller
1959	£618	15s 10d	Convertible
Minor 1000 (1098cc)			
1964	£573	18s 4d	Four-door
1968	£636	0s 0d	Two-door
	£713	0s 0d	Traveller

A Minor 1000 stands quietly in the main street of Burford in Oxfordshire during the summer of 1958.

The British Motor Trade Association estimated that the scheme had helped keep car prices down, and by 1952 was claiming it had saved those fortunate enough to have the cars two hundred million pounds sterling! This was little consolation for those unable to acquire a vehicle of their choice but for those fortunate enough to buy a new car, prices seem very reasonable by today's standards.

Prices in Britain

In 1948, when the new models were announced, the two-door saloon and tourer versions went on sale at the same basic price of £280 in Britain. With Purchase Tax, the price leapt to £358 10s 7d. By 1952, when the four-door model had been in production for two years, its price had risen to £631 10s 0d, and when the Traveller was introduced in 1953 it sold for £622 6s 8d in Deluxe form.

The Taylor family owned a succession of Morris Minors. Pat Taylor is pictured here with 3 HTC in the late 1950s, wearing typical summer clothes of the period.

The accompanying table shows the Minor's showroom prices (without extras) between 1948 and 1968. Fluctuations in Purchase Tax during this period tend to distort prices somewhat and give rise to some anomalies: for instance, a four-door saloon purchased in 1956 would have cost £668 17s 0d, but a comparable Morris 1000 model would have cost a mere £573 18s 4d in 1964.

Supplying dealers often attached a plaque to the dashboard of cars they sold. This is one for the Ercall Garage pictured on pages 51 and 54. The sight of a district nurse with her Minor was commonplace in the 1950s and 1960s when the Minor's popularity was at its peak.

In spite of the inevitable emphasis on export, distribution of vehicles to the extensive UK dealer network was a thriving business even in the early years. Convoys of cars were driven daily from Oxford to dealerships in London and the Home Counties. For those further afield, fleets of car transporters were used.

Dealers and salesmen

Typical of the large Morris dealerships were London-based Stewart and Ardern, Appleyards of Leeds and the Kennings network of garages. All made much of customer service and, in true Nuffield style, support materials were very much in evidence in showrooms and service departments. The corporate image was important even then and it seems that little was left to chance. Mechanics and salesmen alike were expected to maintain high standards, and to aid them in their work a wide range of literature was produced by Nuffield Press.

For the salesmen, easy reference guides to all models were produced annually, and these now provide a vital primary source for information including mechanical specifications, trim options, paint colours, period accessories and prices.

To ensure that no opportunity was missed to inform potential owners of the virtues of all aspects of the Morris Minor, BMC even provided a special 65-point Walk Around Guide for Salesmen. This, no doubt, formed the basis for most of their 'patter' as they took customers around the car. The approved tour started at the front left-hand door handle, and continued in a clockwise direction

First steps: like countless thousands of others in years gone by, this learner driver makes a first hesitant move away from the kerbside in a Birmingham driving school's Morris Minor.

as the salesman pointed out significant features. With the emphasis firmly on 'Quality First', as described in supportive advertising literature, the advantages of the Minor over other contemporary vehicles from rival manufacturers were stressed.

Clearly the strategy worked as sales of the Minor rocketed. Some would say the cars sold themselves, although the sales staff would probably dispute that! The fact remains, however, that demand for the Minor outstripped supply. As export restrictions eased in the late 1950s, home market sales assumed greater significance and during 1960 total sales reached one million for all Morris Minor models – a truly remarkable achievement and a historic landmark for a British car manufacturer.

Personal collection

Waiting lists were not uncommon, though, and in an effort to save a little time and a little money on the overall price, some owners elected to go direct to the factory to collect their cars. Sometimes they did not get the model they originally ordered – a point illustrated by long-time Morris Minor owner, Mike Taylor, who was one of those who went to Cowley to pick up his Morris Minor Saloon in 1958.

In the Ercall Garage's paint shop, a Minor van is finished in the two special colours requested by its new owner.

"I had to wait over a year before I could get the car. In fact when I first placed the order they were making the split-screen version with the 803cc OHV engine. When I was notified that the car was ready, the model had changed and it was the new version – the 948cc Morris 1000 with the one-piece screen. By actually going to Cowley to collect the car personally you could save yourself £5 on the normal price. This particular car was a Deluxe model. It came fitted with overriders and a heater and I specified Connolly leather seats as an extra. These were maroon pleated seats and they complemented the grey colour very well. The car cost £626 plus a few shillings and the odd penny, and the seats were £12 extra.

"The atmosphere at Cowley was very professional – very brisk and business-like. I was at University in Manchester at the time and borrowed a set of trade plates for the day. Most of the other people collecting cars that day were in the trade, and in all there were about thirty people in a reception area, all waiting to collect vehicles. I was in and out within an hour. I didn't have to wait too long before I was taken into the 'delivery room', and there saw the car for the first time. I was very impressed. However, perhaps because I had gone to collect the car myself and because I was using trade plates, I wasn't shown where any of the controls or switches were. Soon I was on the road and, although I was taking the utmost care to run the car in as per the instructions, I was continually being

'pipped' at by the other 'professional' car collectors who were in something of a hurry.

"I had a long journey to make back to Manchester without the aid of motorway and it took me near enough six hours. How times have changed! My only problem was that it began to get dark, and I realised that the instrument panel wasn't illuminated and I didn't know where the switch was. I had to ask a passing motorist for assistance and without further ado I got back to Manchester, well pleased with my new car and very impressed by its performance and

roadholding. I kept the car for two years, during which time I did 42,000 miles in it."

Circumstances conspired to ensure that second-hand prices remained high and owners were encouraged to maintain their Minors very carefully. It was typical of the times that many of them kept meticulous records and adhered rigidly to the recommended servicing schedules. Some examples of these records still survive today, and it is interesting to speculate why they were kept in the first place. Perhaps it had something to do with a habit of careful budgeting stemming from the wartime culture of rationing which continued until 1956, or perhaps it was simply prudent personal financial management.

A Service Voucher system operated and owners were cajoled into having their vehicles inspected every 1000 miles – a far cry from the recommended 10-12,000 mile service intervals of some of the modern cars of today. Morris Motors Ltd and BMC claimed that

Mac Fisheries operated a large fleet of Morris Minor vans with a distinctive blue and white livery.

the Morris Maintenance Voucher system was devised so that vehicles could be maintained in their most efficient and economical running order. In keeping with established practice, the scheme began with a free 500-mile service. The manufacturers claimed with some justification that the car's residual value would be enhanced in the eyes of prospective purchasers if the recommended service intervals were subsequently adhered to.

Fixed price vouchers coupled with locally-based high-profile 'Service Weeks' at main dealerships combined to promote the efficacy of regular maintenance, and all this no doubt contributed to the longevity of many individual vehicles. Fixed charges for repairs with clearly-defined job times provided a clear guide and ensured that customers could budget effectively. There were few hidden charges, but the small print did warn customers that, "Extra work necessary due to rust, seizure of parts or abnormal cleaning; overtime or nightwork; additional road testing prior to or after

Actress Patricia Hayes played the part of a stereotypical elderly Minor owner when she drove this convertible for a 1980 Texaco TV advertisement.

MORRIS MINOR SERIES II & MINOR 1000
SERVICE VOUCHER

1,000 MILES

Servicing Distributor/Dealer _____

_____

Signature _____

_____

_____

...ched by Servicing

MINOR SERIES II & MINOR 1000

MORRIS

A SERVICE VOUCHER **A**

1,000 MILES

This voucher entitles the holder to the service scheduled overleaf at the charge stipulated

DUE WHEN YOUR SPEEDOMETER READS _____

Cost of oil and materials extra

STANDARD **13/-** CHARGE

APPLICABLE IN THE UNITED KINGDOM ONLY

VEHICLES (EXCISE) ACT. 1949.
4634631
EXPIRING 31ST DECEMBER
CX9 592
PRIVATE
MORRIS
£ s. d.
CAP. OR H.P. — 12 10 0
TONS — CWT. —
FOR REFUNDS SEE CONDITIONS ON BACK OF LICENCE.
19 60
29 DEC 59
LICENCE FOR A MECHANICALLY PROPELLED VEHICLE

Some bargains by today's standards – a 1,000-mile service for 13s (65p), annual road tax at £12 10s and fixed-price charges for repairs.

MORRIS

MORRIS MINOR (Series II)
AND
MORRIS MINOR TRAVELLER

SCHEDULE OF REPAIR
AND ADJUSTMENT CHARGES
APPLICABLE TO THE UNITED KINGDOM

Charges revised 1st June, 1955

MORRIS MINOR (Series II) and MINOR TRAVELLER

Operation Number	Description of Operation	Price £ s. d.
	ENGINE	
E.1	Engine only, remove and refit	
E.2	Engine only, remove from frame and fit replacement, changing over all ancillary equipment, including cleaning and adjusting carburetter, distributor and air cleaner	3 19 0
E.3	Engine and gearbox, complete power unit, remove and refit	4 19 0
E.4	Engine and gearbox, remove from frame, fit replacement power unit, changing over all ancillary equipment	5 5 6
E.5	Air cleaner, remove, clean and refit	6 5 6
E.6	Carburetter, adjust mixture	6 6
E.7	Carburetter, remove and refit	3 6
E.8	Carburetter, remove, dismantle and clean, fit new jet washers, reassemble, refit and adjust	6 6
E.9	Connecting rod bearings, remove and refit (one pair)	1 3 0
E.10	Extra per pair	13 0
E.11	Crankshaft and camshaft gears, remove and refit or fit new	3 6
E.12	Crankshaft pulley, fit new	1 13 0
E.13	Cylinder drain tap, remove and refit	1 0 0
E.14	Cylinder head, remove and refit	3 6
E.15	Cylinder head, remove and refit, changing one valve	1 9 6
E.16	Extra per valve	1 13 0
E.17	Extra per valve guide	3 6
		2 0

3

MORRIS MINOR
Facts for Salesmen

YOUR "WALK AROUND" SALES GUIDE

Your "walk around" sales guide. Starting from the left-hand-side front door handle, we walk round the car in a clockwise direction, pointing out the features as we go.

A MAIN SELLING POINTS

1. "Mono - construction." Most modern method of car construction—is stronger, safer, lighter, lasts longer.

2. "Quality First" finish inside and out—degree of finish is remarkably high for price. Six coats of paint, whole body completely rustproofed.

3. Choice of three models— 2-door saloon, 4-door saloon, convertible (lowest priced).

4. Modern, pleasing appearance—no awkward curves not ultra-streamlined. Is a small car with big-car lines.

5. All seats are within the

Publication No. H.5330

wheelbase, for comfort, increased stability and easier driving.

6. Perfect balance—wheelbase, height and track are proportioned correctly.

B UNDER THE BONNET

1. Torsion bar independent front suspension. Permits exceptionally good road-holding and cornering with the most comfortable "ride."

2. Hydraulic piston-type shock absorbers keep the ride smooth.

3. Separate side and headlights. Headlights double-dipping with main beam warning light.

4. 12-volt lighting and ignition system.

5. Rack-and-pinion steering. Very light to handle and extremely accurate—good points with ladies.

6. O.H.V. engine gives good cruising and top-gear performance, improved acceleration and hill climbing.

7. S.U. fuel pump and carburetter—as used on expensive and high-performance cars (Rolls-Royce, Jaguar).

8. Bonnet locks from inside. Double safety-catch at front.

9. Engine accessibility good ; easy access for routine servicing and maintenance. Keeps labour costs down.

10. Good m.p.g. Low overall running costs. Keeps motoring costs as low as possible.

11. Favourable power/weight ratio. Gives good performance and miles per gallon.

12. Lockheed hydraulic four-wheel brakes. Easily adjusted.

C FOR DRIVER & FRONT SEAT PASSENGER

1. Pleasantly styled facia. No ammeter, as C.V.C. is fitted.

2. Parcel tray right across car. Glove box.

3. Front ventilating windows. Open out to act as air scoops in really hot weather.

4. Twin sun visors. Friction

mounting holds them securely in position.

5. Front seat backs tip forward and whole seat lifts forward on 2-door saloon and convertible. Getting in and out is very easy.

6. Door hinges are concealed. Outside door handles are flush-fitting, pull-out type.

7. Headlamp warning signal when lights are not dipped.

8. Green warning light tells when sidelights are on.

9. Twin electric wipers.

10. Four-speed gearbox. Gear lever in central position. Positive in action — no rattles develop.

11. Hand brake cable operates on both rear wheels. Positive in action.

12. Windows wind fully down.

13. Doors have double-action safety lock—good point for children.

14. With 2-door models children can be carried in back securely—cannot get at door handles whilst travelling.

15. Ashtray in centre of facia panel.

16. Heater and radio can easily be fitted.

17. 4-door saloon has interior light.

18. Front seats adjustable.

19. Easy car to drive. Small turning circle, compact overall size allow easy parking, garaging and manœuvrability in traffic.

20. Doors hinged on forward pillars—safety factor if opened inadvertently whilst travelling.

21. Clear driving vision. Driver sits well up. Slender corner and door pillars eliminate blind spots.

22. 4-door saloon has automatic time control switch for trafficators.

23. 4-door saloon has leather upholstery for front seats.

24. Spring steering wheel, horn switch in centre.

25. Foot dipping switch, leaving hands free.

26. Full - width one - piece bumper.

D FOR REAR SEAT PASSENGERS

1. Sit forward of the rear axle.

2. Hypoid rear axle. Silent operation and long life. Permits a low floor.

3. Full - width parcel shelf behind rear seat.

4. Good elbow room and leg room for rear passengers—44 in. (112 cm.) both measurements.

5. Head room ample, consistent with low overall height of car.

6. Convertible rear side windows are permanent. No side screens to stow or crack.

7. 4-door saloon has stainless steel window frames and armrests on rear doors.

---

repair; or extra time taken on road tests at speed outside a congested city area", would all be subject to additional charges.

Owners' endorsements of the Minor

Almost inevitably, owners extolled the virtues of their cars. Many insisted that the Minor lived up to all the claims of the publicity, and wrote to the editors of established motoring magazines and to the Nuffield organisation itself to express their satisfaction.

Commercial and fleet users

The versatility of the Traveller, van and pick-up variants was a major factor in persuading fleet managers to acquire Morris Minors for commercial use. Apart from the public service vehicles (see the next chapter), the sheer variety of companies which used Minors for deliveries, service vehicles, agricultural and building work says much for their practicality. Many fleet users appreciated the uncomplicated nature of the mechanical specifications, citing ease of maintenance and the Minor's unrivalled economy and performance as influential factors in their decision to buy. The variety of options available when buying a van or pick-up also

proved significant, as many companies elected to fit their own custom-built back on to the chassis and cab. Others, like Currys, the High Street electrical retailer, chose to adapt the existing coachwork by adding a high-topped rear section so that the vans could carry the latest upright fridge-freezers.

In the late 1990s, commercial variants are still enjoying a new lease of life. Many of course were well used and have long since been scrapped or abandoned, but considerable numbers survive and increasingly these are being pressed into service in much the same way as they were 30-40 years ago. Some present-day business users – with an eye for promotion and advertising – favour the Minor because of its enduring character and popularity, and the way it conveniently lends itself to effective signwriting.

B.M.C. service in EUROPE

Available to qualified owners of cars manufactured by B.M.C. touring the Continent of Europe against payment in Sterling Vouchers

With a 62-point guide, salesmen were well placed to extol the virtues of the Morris Minor, and for the owner who planned to travel abroad there was a reassuring list of BMC garages outside Britain.

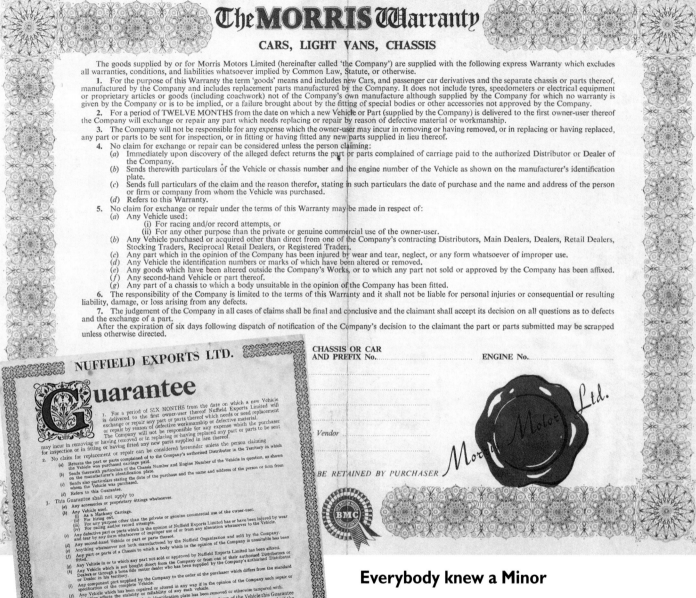

Customers at home and abroad could buy with confidence, knowing their vehicle was backed by a Morris Warranty or a Nuffield Exports Guarantee.

Everybody knew a Minor

So many people seem to have had associations with the Morris Minor, and any present owner will testify that people willingly volunteer information about family or personal associations with the marque. Countless thousands of people have learnt to drive in a Morris Minor, and many people claim that the Minor was their first car; the author is among them. It is interesting to note that in 1997 the Minor was voted 'Classic Car of the Year' and that in the classic car press it is continually recommended as an ideal first classic car.

In modern Britain, where the notion of a classless society is

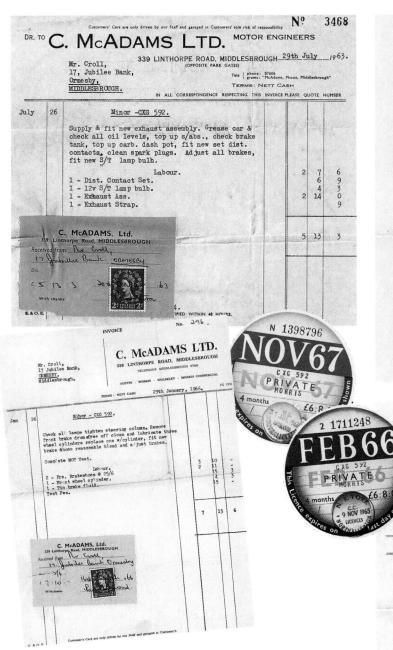

Documents like these
add value and interest
for today's purchasers,
keen to discover more
about the individual
history of their cars.

regularly promoted, the Morris Minor would be a strong contender for 'Car of the People'. Its stereotypical image as the vehicle most frequently used by vicars, district nurses and elderly people in general has given way since production ended to an image of the car with universal appeal. As such, the Minor looks set to attract a whole generation of new owners who will continue to enjoy the pleasure of driving a car which has stood the test of time and been driven billions of miles by millions of people – all over the world.

THE MINOR AT WORK

The enduring popularity of the Morris Minor is due in part to its familiarity to the British public. Like the distinctive red telephone boxes, the humble Morris Minor mail van and GPO Engineers' van were as much a part of everyday life in the 1950s and 1960s as the Bobby on the beat – until he too succumbed to the charms of the dependable Minor, and Morris Minor Panda cars became the order of the day.

Post Office vans

The introduction of the Morris Minor Commercial Range in 1953 signalled the beginning of a new era for the Post Office, which had long been a staunch user of Morris products. Over the next few years, its Morris Z Type vans were phased out in favour of the new O Type Series II Morris Minor van. Apart from a brief flirtation with Ford Anglia vans in the mid-1960s, the GPO's loyalty to the Morris marque remained unquestioned, and the Minor saw service for more than 20 years. In that time a total of 52,745 vehicles were produced for contracts which were tightly costed and resulted in specifications which made these service vehicles radically different from standard production light commercials.

Perhaps the most radical of them all were the first Royal Mail and GPO Engineers' vans, which were fitted with rubber front wings! These specially moulded wings were similar in shape and design to the earlier Series MM front wings, but the headlamps were externally mounted on top – no doubt a carry-over from Z Type

The GPO mail and telephone engineers' vans were built to a specification distinctively different from that of the standard Morris Minor light commercials.

The 'postie' in his smart uniform was a familiar sight in Britain, as often as not accompanied by his Minor van. Such vans remained in service from 1953 to 1975.

With their distinctive yellow livery, the last of the Post Office Telephones vans certainly made an impression – even if the colour was not to everyone's liking.

days. The GPO believed that the rubber wings would more easily absorb the impact of a collision, and that repair bills would be correspondingly reduced.

Low unit costs were reflected in other cost-cutting features. The traditional metal facia panel was replaced by a painted wooden board and a basic first aid kit was attached to this where the passenger glove box lid would otherwise have been. A heater was considered to be an extravagant extra, and so an opening windscreen was fitted to aid ventilation and to prevent misting up. Roof-mounted wipers had to be fitted to suit this arrangement. As daily workhorses, the GPO vans were expected to endure rough treatment, and so rubber matting was fitted to the driver's compartment. Even this wore out, and after 1959 special-issue GPO heavy-duty link type matting was used.

Rubber wings were a novel feature of early Post Office vehicles. The rationale behind their fitting was that minor impacts would not cause damage.

As if all this was not enough, the Mail vans also had only one seat fitted. A passenger seat was always an optional extra on Morris commercials, and the GPO decided to manage without. Instead, the space created was used as additional storage for letters and parcels. However, passenger seats were usually specified for the

Minor vans supplied to GPO from 1953 to 30.9.69	
Red Postal (Royal Mails)	18,431
Green telephone (the last 1,500 of these were yellow)	21,256
Red Postal Engineering	55
Minor vans supplied to Post Office Corporation from 1.10.69	
Red Postal (Royal Mails)	6,401
Yellow telephone	6,410
Red Postal Engineering	192
Grand total	**52,745**

Inspectors' vehicles, which were used for visiting Post Offices, and always for Driving Instructor Vans. Examples of these remained in service right to the end of production.

Neither Mail nor Engineers' vans normally strayed far from where they were based, and so the Post Office saw no need for the extra performance offered by the 948cc engine when it became available. Consequently, no GPO vehicles ever had that engine, and all new vehicles delivered before 1964 had the 803cc 'Series II' type. Subsequent deliveries had the 1098cc engine – but even that was a special variety (designated 10 MC) fitted with a speed governor. Perhaps this was why there is no record of any GPO van taking part in a high-speed chase after a Post Office robbery!

Nevertheless, the GPO was alert to the need for security, and adopted several special measures on both Royal Mail and GPO Engineers' vehicles. Wire mesh was fitted on the rear door windows of both types, and the telephone engineers' vans had a wooden-framed wire mesh partition to separate the cab from the rest of the body. On mail vans, a half-height partition behind the driver's seat

Nothing was too much trouble, as illustrated by this picture of a delivery van making its way to one of the Scottish islands on its daily round. The L-plate in the rear window suggests that the van may also have been used to teach a new recruit how to drive.

protected him from objects in the rear thrown forward under braking. The driver of a Royal Mail van could also lock the rear doors from his seat, by operating a hand lever which activated a steel bar; telephone engineers' vans, however, had only a hasp and padlock in addition to the standard rear door handle.

Perhaps the most unconventional security device ever fitted to a vehicle was introduced on the Minor mail vans in 1957. This was developed in response to a request from the GPO by Reg Job, one of the original Minor design team. By fitting a Yale lock strategically beneath the quarter light and forward of the main window glass on both driver and passenger doors, he ensured that the door automatically locked on closing. In so doing he also simplified things for the driver who, on returning to his vehicle, simply used the Yale lock to activate a rod mechanism which then allowed the normal door handle to be used. Unfortunately, the system also had one drawback. Post Office employee Bob Logan was a regular driver of Morris Minor mail vans from 1966 to 1973, and he recalls that the automatic locking system caught out many drivers who had to

Whatever the weather, strenuous efforts were made to get deliveries through, as this scene in Scotland illustrates. There were no heaters in these early 1960s vans!

Throughout the length and breadth of the UK, daily deliveries of the mail led to the 'postie' becoming a vital part of community life. The Minor vans were referred to by the Post Office as '50 cubic-foot' types.

Bob Logan's mail round was in Uxbridge, Middlesex, and he used this delivery van until 1970 when it was replaced by a second Minor, registered FYD 715J. Like many postmen, Bob learned to drive in a week, in a Post Office Driving Instructor's van!

In response to the bi-lingual lobby, Welsh Mail vans adopted bi-lingual lettering carrying the words 'Post Brenhinol' in addition to 'ROYAL MAIL' in 1969. In the case of Telephone Engineers' vans, a system similar to that adopted by the Scots was the order of the day: vans carried only a Royal Crown with the words 'Post Office Telephones' and the name of the district where the van was based. However, on the last of the deliveries of vans to Wales, the words 'Post Office Telephones' were replaced with the image of a telephone handset.

A final variation emerged in 1981 when British Telecom became separate from the Post Office, and the last telephone engineers' Minors in service sported their distinctive yellow livery and the words 'British Telecom' with details of the district. These vans closed an era of active service and a happy association with the Post Office and its successors which had prompted other countries to adopt the Minor as their main vehicle for postal deliveries. Apart from the Isle of Man, Jersey and Guernsey, the Bahamian and Turkish Post Offices also had fleets of Minors.

A final note of distinction rests with these popular vehicles. The main production of Mail and Engineers' vans moved from Cowley in the early 1960s to Adderley Park, Birmingham, and it was here that the last Minor was produced. Although production records have been lost, it is believed that the last Minor to be produced was a Royal Mail van. Officially, production is thought to have ended in December 1971, although the Post Office did take delivery of a batch of vans in February 1972. The last van – chassis number 327369 – was in active service in Dorchester until 1979 when it was sold at auction. As happened with all Post Office vehicles, it was first stripped of its special lettering, Royal Crests, wire mesh and other special equipment. Intriguingly, a mystery surrounds the fate of this final production Morris Minor.

Police Minors

Although the Post Office was undoubtedly the largest fleet user of Morris Minors, many other County, Metropolitan, Municipal Borough and District Authorities took Morris Minors into their vehicle fleets. As a result, Minors also found their way into the hands of Police forces, where they enjoyed a distinguished career – particularly in the late 1960s and early 1970s.

Norfolk County Council used Nuffield products exclusively in the late 1940s and early 1950s, and it is no surprise to find that

face the embarrassment of being locked out of their own vehicles!

The GPO used distinctive signwriting on its vehicles in each of the four home nations, and restorers nowadays seek special permission to use the proper insignia, to achieve an authentic appearance for their vehicles. Mail vans used in England, Wales and Northern Ireland displayed the words 'ROYAL MAIL' along with a Royal Crown and Elizabeth II's initials. Those used in Scotland, on the other hand, displayed only the words 'ROYAL MAIL' and a slightly larger Scottish Crown but without the Monarch's initials. This difference results from the Scots' reluctance to recognise Elizabeth I as Queen: while they fully accept the sovereignty of the present Monarch, they see her as Elizabeth I and not Elizabeth II! So to avoid confusion, any direct reference to Her Majesty was removed from the insignia.

Norfolk was one of the first Police forces to use the Morris Minor, and these WPCs are pictured alongside their car in 1949. Photographed in 1992, the last Minor in active Police use was based at Port Stanley in the Falkland Islands.

One of the last Panda cars to be ordered was this one, which was purchased in 1971 by the Devon and Cornwall Constabulary from local dealers Mumford's. It saw service as a Unit Beat car until 1974, when it was acquired by its present owner who has carefully restored it. Note how its livery differs slightly from that on the Lothian and Peebles cars (overleaf), which had a white band on the roof as well as white doors.

The advent of Unit Beat Policing in the 1960s brought the Minor to prominence as a Police vehicle. Fleets of Panda cars were ordered by forces throughout the UK; these belonged to the Lothian and Peebles Constabulary, and were pictured on being taken into service.

one of the earliest recorded uses of a Minor by the Police was in this county, where a black two-door saloon entered service during 1949. In the years that followed, many other Police forces followed suit. Some early Morris 1000 vans were used as Dog Handlers' vehicles, while other variants were used as Forensic and Scene of Crime vehicles. In some forces, the versatile Morris 1000 Traveller models were acquired for the exclusive use of Police photographers.

However, it was the introduction of Unit Beat Policing in the late 1960s which really brought the Morris Minor to prominence as a Police vehicle. The concept had come to fruition in Lancashire in 1965 when Panda cars were introduced on a trial basis in the town of Kirkby. So successful was the scheme that it was extended to the whole of the county within two years. Other forces soon followed suit and Panda cars, so called because of their unusual two-tone colour scheme, became firmly established throughout the British Isles. Two types became widespread: the Ford Anglia 105E and the Morris Minor.

The Morris Minor Panda cars were usually two-door Morris 1000 Saloons – favoured by the police because their 'clients' would have great difficulty making an escape once installed in the back seat. Panda cars were normally painted blue and white, and Minors commonly had their doors and that part of the roof forward of the B-posts in white while the remainder of the vehicle was in Bermuda Blue. Seating was of standard design, although the driver's seat was specially strengthened to cope with the increased use it would inevitably have. Interiors were usually black, although some were red. A special zipped headlining was also fitted to allow ready access

to the wiring for the roof-mounted illuminated 'POLICE' sign. Later Police cars had alternators fitted and some had more accurately calibrated speedometers. The *Rochdale Observer* noted that the town's seven new Panda cars (KDF 523F to KDF 529F) which entered service on March 1st, 1968, also carried a traffic cone, flashing beacons, first aid kits and a personal radio to connect the patrol with the Officer in charge.

D-Day – delivery day for a new fleet of Morris Minor Panda cars – was always a memorable occasion, and many forces marked the event with what would now be termed a photo opportunity. Rochdale certainly did so, and so did the Lothian and Peebles Constabulary in Scotland when they adopted Unit Beat Policing in the Counties of East Lothian, Mid Lothian, West Lothian and Peebleshire during 1969. To mark the introduction of their 20-strong fleet of sequentially registered Pandas, a special inaugural event was held at Dalkeith Police Station. Records also show that the Police in Devon and Cornwall were still buying Minor Panda cars from local dealers as late as July 1971, some eight months after production of two-door saloons ended.

Minors served Police forces well, and many were used in other capacities than Panda cars. Stockport Borough Police used four distinctively liveried Morris Minor Courtesy Cars on an experimental basis, the idea being to improve relations between motorists and the police. With three large chevrons painted on their bonnets, there would be no mistaking who was behind you when you chanced to look in your rear-view mirror!

Other Morris Minors, including four-door saloons, vans and

Travellers continued to be used by the police, and London's Metropolitan Police were major fleet buyers. Most of these vehicles were finished in standard colours, Trafalgar Blue being the most popular. Exceptions included the Edinburgh Police who had a number of Panda-liveried Travellers, the Thames Valley Police who used black Travellers as regular transport for CID officers, the Gateshead Constabulary who operated a small fleet of dark blue Dog Handlers' vans, and the Wiltshire Police who had the most outrageously liveried green vans which sported mustard yellow doors and signwritten panels with a blue flashing light on the roof.

The Police Minors were sold on after their useful service life, and many still survive and are eagerly sought by some enthusiasts. However, for longevity in active service the accolades go far beyond the shores of Britain to the South Atlantic: Port Stanley in the Falkland Islands had a white Morris Minor still in active service as late as 1992!

Military Minors

The Morris 1000 Traveller was used extensively by all three sections of the British Armed Forces, both in Britain and abroad. When introduced in 1966, it replaced the Standard Ensign and the Hillman Husky. Its duties involved a wide variety of technical and administrative tasks, although primary functions included the

A rare photograph of a military Minor on active service: bomb disposal officers are defusing an unexploded wartime German 250kg bomb. The 'Bomb Disposal' Traveller was used to transport the initial response team to such finds.

movement of light goods and personnel. Military records indicate that the Morris Traveller was used by Chaplains, staff at Careers Information and Recruitment Offices, Education Departments, District Headquarters and by mobile display teams.

More technical functions were carried out by those vehicles which were classified as operational. Perhaps the most unusual were the Bomb Disposal Travellers. Long-standing bomb disposal officer Major (Retd.) A.S. Hoben QGM remembers well how the Morris Traveller was deployed and the distinguishing features of this special vehicle:

> *"The Morris 1000 Traveller was regularly used to carry the initial response team of an officer, a senior NCO or Warrant Officer and their equipment to UK bomb sites. The vehicle was painted olive green with the front wings painted pillar box red. A sign board on the roof immediately above the windscreen and another across the two rear doors were painted white with red letters spelling 'BOMB DISPOSAL' or occasionally 'ROYAL ENGINEER BOMB DISPOSAL' in two lines. The vehicle was also fitted with a blue flashing light mounted on the centre of the roof".*

Other specialist roles for the Minor included use by the Military Police and various engineering units. The RAF deployed examples for use by aircraft servicing and repair teams and for general use on airfields, while the Royal Navy vehicles were used by Naval Police at dockyards and as staff cars by Senior Officers of Aircraft Carriers. Morris Travellers were taken on board and used as

The Army's Morris Traveller models were painted in the traditional British military dark green. This was one of a large batch ordered in 1969 and was pictured at the Royal Norfolk Showground in June 1974. Just over a year later, it was withdrawn from service. Note how the wood has been painted to match the bodywork, although this was not standard on military Travellers. These Travellers had a basic interior specification which included a one-piece rubber mat and plain door trims.

The RAF also used Travellers. Like this one, many of them were bought at auction after they were decommissioned and are still in everyday use after re-registration as civilian vehicles in the year of their release – but this car retains its original RAF registration plates.

British military Minors had identification plates like this one fixed to the glovebox lid. An additional identification plate, again unique to the military, was attached to the engine side of the bulkhead.

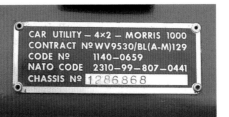

regular transport when the ships docked. Which parts of the Empire saw these vehicles on active service must remain a subject for speculation, although it is clear that a substantial number of Travellers were used in service in Cyprus, Malta, Gibraltar and Hong Kong. Those designated for use in Germany were supplied with left-hand drive and were used extensively by the Royal Corps of Transport as well as by soldiers and civilians as personal transport.

Between 1966 and 1971 Morris Travellers were supplied to the British Armed Services under at least 15 contracts. There were 2048 vehicles in all, of which 1776 were used by the Army. Of these, 746 had left-hand drive and went to BAOR (British Army of the Rhine) in Germany. A further 217 were allocated to the RAF, and of these 81 were sent to Cyprus. The Royal Navy had a relatively small contingent of 55 vehicles. All these vehicles were distributed to their units from Central Vehicle Depots at Hilton, Ashchurch and Irvine in the UK, and at Antwerp in Belgium.

As was to be expected, standard military colours were adopted for Army and RAF vehicles. The Army vehicles were painted Army Bronze Green, and those for the RAF in that service's characteristic Blue-Grey. However, the Royal Navy's Minors were not finished in that service's traditional Navy Blue but were supplied in the black used for personnel transport vehicles. Additional variations in colour schemes included the Bomb Disposal vehicles, those allocated to airfield duties (which had prominent yellow markings to aid visibility) and vehicles serving in the tropics (which were painted all-over white).

Minors used by Government and Local Authority Departments

The list of Government and Local Authority Departments which used Morris Minors is too extensive to cover in detail. HM Customs and Excise, the Department of the Environment (Property Services Agency), the Ministry of Agriculture and the Department of

Health and Social Security were all among those who used Morris Minor cars and vans.

Health Boards allocated cars for the use of district nurses and Midwives, and some Social Services Departments provided specially adapted Disabled Persons' Vehicles. These varied in the extent to which they were modified for their eventual owners, but they were supplied on contract to a basic non-standard specification. The earliest contracts which were issued in the late 1950s for Morris 1000 Saloons were fulfilled with vehicles which had the earlier Series II 803cc engine and transmission. The earlier type of badging and Series II carpeting were also used, but the principal concession to the disabled users were specially designed front seats. These were mounted on runners which allowed for easier adjustment and improved access.

Later contracts for Disabled Persons' cars continued to call for two-door saloons, and these had standard mechanical specification which included the 1098cc engine. The main differences from standard vehicles were in the interior, where plain door and side trims, specially adjustable front seats and provision for a fire extinguisher set these vehicles apart from other Minors.

Indian taxis

Morris Minors have served the public well, but few perhaps have served it as well as the taxis which ply their trade on the Indian sub-continent. Thousands of Morris Minors have endured the rigours of the demanding road network, tested the ingenuity of panel beaters and mechanics alike, and provided nostalgic trips for tourists and regular transport for local people for decades.

In Sri Lanka, yellow-topped Minor taxis are as much a part of everyday life in the 1990s as they were when the Minor was the best-selling car on the island 40 years ago. According to Ranjan Canekeratne, the Minor was limited in its usefulness as a taxi because in its original form as a Series II four-door saloon it could only accommodate three passengers. However, at his behest the rear seat backrest was moved forward by four inches and the rear wheel arches were padded sufficiently to allow for a seat width of 45 inches – enough to accommodate an extra passenger! The rest is now history, and the Minor looks set to defy all the odds and continue as a public service vehicle for some time yet – unless BBC reporter Brian Barron's fears are realised and demand once more increases for Morris Minor steering columns to use as gun barrels!

A number of aftermarket controls to suit disabled drivers were available for the Morris Minor. This system by Feeny and Johnson was designed for a driver who had lost the use of his legs, and is still fitted to a 1956 Series II saloon.

This Indian taxi driver stands proudly by his Morris Minor taxi in Colombo, Sri Lanka. His clothing is nicely colour-coordinated with the car!

PERIOD EXTRAS AND ACCESSORIES

Following the merger between Austin and Morris to form BMC, Approved Accessories were heavily promoted and salesmen were given a comprehensive pocket guide packed full of information for customers. All accessories carried 12 months' warranty.

Electric Mirror Clock
For double convenience this small electric clock is set in a tinted anti-glare mirror and is fitted in the normal interior mirror position of any car. The dial of the clock can be illuminated at night.

Electric Clock
The correct time when you want it, where you want it. This clock is operated by electrical impulses and its time-keeping is therefore constant and accurate.

Vanity Mirror
A particularly useful addition to the car's equipment, especially for the ladies. Quickly and unobtrusively attached to the rear of the sun visor, ready in an instant for those vital adjustments to personal appearances.

Interior Prismatic Mirror
At a touch this mirror eliminates the blinding reflection of the car lights behind, yet gives a secondary image of the following traffic without glare or interference. It can be fitted in place of the normal driving mirror.

Issigonis disapproved of reclining seats like these offered as an optional extra for late Minor 1000 models. In his view, 'drivers should be encouraged to adopt an upright driving position, not to lie down.'

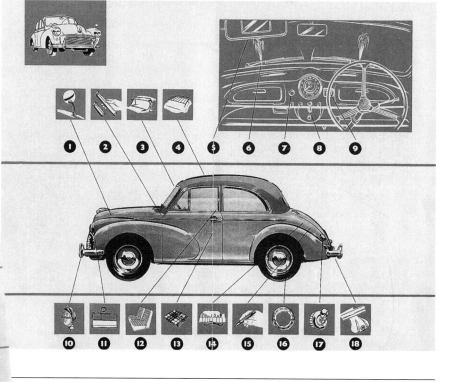

A full range of accessories approved by the engineers who developed and produced the Morris Minor was effectively marketed through simply-designed brochures. This one dates from 1960.

MORRIS MINOR 1000

ACCESSORIES

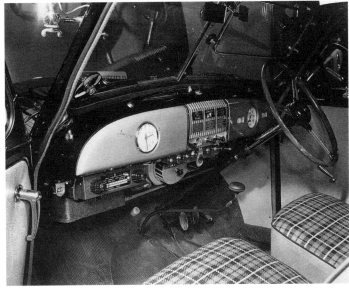

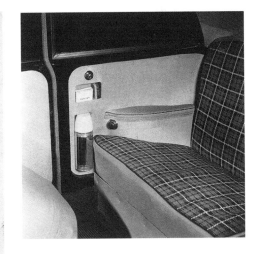

Of course you'll want radio in your new Morris…

THE NUFFIELD ORGANISATION

exclusively fits and recommends

"HIS MASTER'S VOICE" *car-planned* AUTOMOBILE RADIO

and has made special provision for it in the new

MORRIS MINOR and MORRIS OXFORD

These illustrations show how neatly and unobtrusively "His Master's Voice" Automobile Radio fits into the new MORRIS range as an *integral part* of these fine cars.

★ A WORD OF EXPLANATION

"His Master's Voice" Automobile Radio is the joint product of The Gramophone Company Ltd. and Smiths Motor Accessories Ltd., who have combined to form *Radiomobile Limited*. The world-wide resources of the two parent companies have enabled *Radiomobile Limited* to establish a network of Overseas Distributors, offering unequalled sales and service facilities.

RADIOMOBILE LTD., CRICKLEWOOD WORKS, LONDON, N.W.2

"HIS MASTER'S VOICE" AUTOMOBILE RADIO

PRODUCT OF

RADIOMOBILE

Britain's automobile radio specialists

Morris Motors recommended the Radiomobile 'His Master's Voice' radio in spite of Issigonis's view that it represented a 'distraction to the driver'. In 1948, its £42 price tag represented more than 10% of the purchase price of a new Morris Minor!

This special car bedecked with every conceivable extra dates from 1953. Once dubbed 'the poor man's Rolls-Royce', the humble Morris Minor had broad appeal.

For convertible owners, the Hodscren rear window provided vastly improved vision out of the back.

At least two hard-top conversions were offered during the mid-fifties. The one by Airflow Streamlines Ltd of Northampton cost £89 in 1955, and that pictured – made by C.L. Potter and sold under the Westmoreland brand name – cost just £39.

Some aftermarket accessories dramatically changed the appearance of the Minor. These American-style 'fender skirts' were manufactured by Appleyards of Leeds, a big Nuffield and Morris dealership, but did not prove popular and are rare today.

The 'Tourer-to-Coupé' conversion (above) marketed by Jarvis and Sons fundamentally changed the appearance of the car. Sales material stressed improved security, which was a valid point in view of the flimsiness of the original sidescreens.

Among the most popular aftermarket accessories were these 'sill finishers'.

Alexander Engineering of Haddenham in Buckinghamshire were better known for their engine modifications than for this unique glass fibre replacement boot lid which was supplied in primer. It offered a major increase in luggage capacity, but its lines did not harmonise too well with the car's existing styling.

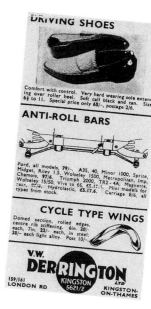

Whitewall tyres were most commonly associated with American cars in the fifties, but many European makers offered them as an optional extra to cash in on the vogue for all things American. They are seen here on a Dutch-registered low-light Minor.

The standard Morris Minor handled well and was widely praised for that, but Derrington found a ready market for these effective anti-roll bars. Satisfied customer Bob Perry fitted his in 1970, and 200,000 miles later believes it was the best £6.50 he ever spent and the best Minor modification ever offered!

Faster warm-up in cold weather was promised by the Muffette. Such accessories were popular in the fifties and sixties.

These American Amco bars offered additional protection in the case of low-speed impacts. They are seen fitted to a British-registered car which has been exported to an enthusiastic owner in the USA and retains its original number plate under the American one!

EPIC JOURNEYS BY MINOR

Morris Motors Limited had a stringent testing regime for new models and the Minor in all its guises was subjected to the rigours of this. Extensive trials at the factory proving ground at Chalgrove Airfield provided many hair-raising experiences as well as a wealth of valuable technical information on all aspects of design and engineering. It was Morris policy that all new models should cover 10,000 miles without problems – not much by modern standards, but a lot of miles then – and this ensured that experienced teams of testers were kept fully employed driving the cars of the future, mainly in England but occasionally abroad. Even the chief designer, Alec Issigonis, took his turn at the wheel to ensure that the prototype Mosquito with its experimental flat-four engine was put through its paces.

Outside the factory, motoring journalists and professional road-testers of course investigated and challenged the manufacturer's claims for new models. So the Minor was subjected to a number of long-haul tests, many of them designed to establish how practical and dependable the car was in a variety of situations. In every case, the car came through with flying colours and was praised in print.

The Monte Carlo press car, 1949

The Autocar's redoubtable reporter Sammy Davis set the tone soon after the Minor entered production. Using the very first two-door saloon to come off the assembly line, he set out on a well-publicised 1600-mile trip to the French Riviera with Monte Carlo as the main destination. An added bonus was that the itinerary would include most of the Monte Carlo Rally route – and the car would be used as regular transport for the duration of the event.

Northern France presented an early challenge for the Minor, with wartime destruction still very much in evidence in Calais and Boulogne, and the roads in a poor state. The Minor was undeterred,

however, the verdict being that it might have been made for the job; suspension and handling came in for special praise. On the route of the rally, the car excelled again, and "even allowing for the absence of snow and ice," reported Davis, "the car was ahead of schedule by some two minutes on the upward climb to the final pass and thirteen minutes early on the downward leg to Grasse".

On a test of 658 miles out of a total of 1697 miles covered, the Minor averaged 38mpg and oil consumption was negligible. Luggage accommodation was found to be startling and the rear seats quite comfortable, while handling was magnificent and the suspension excellent. In terms of value for money, the car was regarded as being "in a class of its own". The only down-side of the trip was a small accident in dense fog on the rally route, when the French driver of a Hillman attempted a crazy overtaking manoeuvre while the Morris was already overtaking another vehicle. In spite of the awful noise from the inevitable collision, damage to the first production Minor was limited to two dents on the car's wings.

To Switzerland with Ian Appleyard, 1949

Both *The Autocar* and *The Motor* reported many other notable journeys in Europe featuring early Morris Minors. In the spring of 1949, *The Motor's* Joseph Lowrey and photographer Louis Klemantaski joined forces with international rally driver Ian Appleyard for a weekend jaunt to Switzerland.

Appleyard of course had access to a whole range of vehicles, because he was a director of the family firm Appleyards of Leeds, who were major Morris Distributors. His plan was to convince his press colleagues that 1600 miles in a weekend was a viable option in a compact small car, and to that end he chose the new Minor. The example he chose was a demonstrator model registered MNW 970, which earned it the nickname of the 'Minnow'. Even though the

The Autocar *borrowed a Minor for their coverage of the 1949 Monte Carlo Rally, and the one which Morris Motors lent them was the first production example, NWL 576.*

car had only 2000 miles on its clock, Appleyard's careful preparation included a decoke.

Appleyard's proposed itinerary for a trip to Geneva which would combine business with pleasure was viewed with some scepticism, particularly as it was designed to indulge his other passion of skiing. As a member of the British Olympic Ski team, he had scheduled a stop at the challenging Jura Slopes! Nevertheless, after a Friday departure from Leeds and a stop in London to collect the other crew members, the schedule was maintained and the twin objectives of attending the Geneva Motor Show and skiing on the Jura slopes were achieved. The projected arrival time in London – 9am on Monday – was met with three minutes to spare, and this after an unscheduled visit to Paris. The car performed impeccably throughout, returning excellent mpg and delighting its trio of drivers with its superb road-holding and unfussy progress.

A Minor on the Icknield Way, 1951

One of the most memorable journeys undertaken in a Morris Minor in Britain covered just 52 miles and was undertaken in 1951. Covering the sort of terrain better suited to a modern four-wheel drive vehicle, the Minor ploughed across the Icknield Way, an ancient route which runs across Britain from Norfolk to the West Country, pre-dates Roman roads and was then estimated to have been in use for 2000 years.

It was E.H. Row of *The Motor* who persuaded the Nuffield organisation to provide a Series MM Tourer on loan for the trip, in spite of warnings that almost anything could happen to it. The venture aimed to refute the suggestion that "a modern, quantity produced car with independent front suspension, unit construction and enveloping coachwork was less capable of 'taking a bashing' than its earlier counterpart!". At least, that was the official line – but the prospect of an amusing day's out-of-the-ordinary motoring counted for just as much.

Given that the Icknield Way was no more than a drovers' track – upgraded only in parts to metalled road – and that parts were 'lost', this was a truly daunting challenge. To add weight to the venture, a photographer and two friends were added to the crew, and their presence was to prove invaluable because three weeks of almost continuous rain had made the proposed route treacherous and in parts almost impassable.

After a start at Wallingford, just off the London to Oxford road, the going was good for the first few miles. However, the fun began once the narrow metalled lane came to an abrupt end. The first precaution was to reduce the pressure in the rear tyres from 28psi to 17psi, to cope with the going which was by now "very soft". Extra weight concentrated on the rear seat helped as the Minor charged through deep ruts full of mud and water. At one stage water poured into the car when a door was opened.

Conditions became worse as the journey progressed with only occasional respite when parts of the way were metalled, but the car coped admirably. At one point the Minor was "forcing its way along a muddy strip with twigs and branches brushing the hood and sides of the car. Each time an overhead branch loomed up the crew instinctively ducked in unison". Conditions were to worsen still further, and the car faced greater trials by mud and water:

The last mile of original trackway gave the Minor the worst hammering of the whole trip. On an up gradient all the way, and with a wet, grassy surface, it was criss-crossed with a multitude of fairly deep cross gullies, practically impossible to avoid. So, with the crew keeping their heads down and hanging on like grim death, this section was taken as fast as possible, for the light was failing and we had no wish to stop again. One moment the car was airborne; the next it would crash down with a thud that shook everything and everybody, really giving the suspension something to get on with. Yet, when we ultimately reached hard going and Baldock, there was nothing apart from a coating of mud, the broken headlamp and sundry scratches on the coachwork to show what the Minor had been through. Indeed, as one of the crew remarked as we bowled home down the A1, "You'd think the little blighter had never been outside Hyde Park in its life".

Praise indeed, but history does not record whether the car was returned to the factory fully valeted inside and out!

The Trans-Saharan Expedition, 1952

The durability of the Series MM Morris Minor was further tested with trips much further afield. In 1952 an incredible Trans-Saharan Expedition was undertaken by two Ulstermen, brothers James and Boyd Baird. Against all the odds, they drove a second-hand 1949 Series MM Saloon with 28,000 miles on the clock all the way from Girelo in Southern Rhodesia to Belfast in Northern Ireland, where they planned a family visit.

The Baird brothers trusted to the reliability of the Morris and left the car in standard form, the only modification being roof-

mounted storage tanks for petrol and drinking water. However, the 44-gallon capacity of these seriously affected the power-to-weight ratio, and petrol consumption significantly increased – particularly on the desert stage where a lot of low gear work was required as the car repeatedly got stuck in the soft sandy conditions. Home comforts were few and far between for the crew. During their 9000-mile trip they slept in the car every night, with a single exception when they accepted hospitality offered by missionaries.

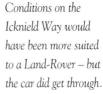

Conditions on the Icknield Way would have been more suited to a Land-Rover – but the car did get through.

The Baird brothers reach Nuffield Exports in Oxford, close to the end of their Trans-Saharan Expedition. Countries visited on the 9000-mile trip are painted on the battered car.

One of the stars of the 1952 Nuffield organisation film, Dusty Miles, *was this Series MM Tourer, photographed against the backdrop of a traditional American riverboat.*

The marathon journey took them through Northern Rhodesia, the Belgian Congo, across French Equatorial Africa and the Cameroons before reaching Kano in northern Nigeria. Next came the arduous crossing of the Sahara Desert, after which the brothers were able to claim an unusual record because their Morris Minor became the smallest car to successfully conquer the Hoggar Mountain route in the desert. After the Saharan crossing, the brothers headed for the port of Algiers and made a sea crossing to Marseilles. A leisurely trip through France followed, and then they headed for England where they impressed the staff at Nuffield Export Headquarters in Oxford with tales of their exploits. The final leg of their journey took them to Scotland and then Ireland for

a family visit, after which they returned to Rhodesia, taking the car with them. On this occasion, however, they travelled by sea!

The Alaskan Highway, 1952

North America provided some of the most spectacular scenery for a truly epic journey when the Nuffield organisation made a promotional film entitled *Dusty Miles* in 1952 to demonstrate the sturdy reliability of the Minor. Set in the picturesque landscape of Alaska, British Columbia and the Yukon, the film charted the course of the Alaskan Highway, a new 1525-mile road built in 1942 when America was preparing for the possibility of invasion.

Through the efforts of 10,000 American and Canadian soldiers and 6000 civilians, the route through virgin territory to create a new supply line had been completed in seven months at the rate of eight miles a day. This so-called 'Miracle Road' traversed a number of natural obstacles including lakes, rivers and swamps, and passed through regions of America which are now part of folklore, including Indian Territory and Gold Rush towns.

The stars of the film were a pair of high-headlamp Series MM Morris Minors, one a tourer and the other a saloon. Each car covered 3000 miles in the course of making the film, performing admirably and coping with a mixture of terrain which ranged from

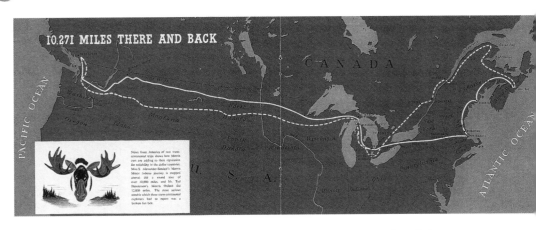

Culture clash: inquisitive members of the North American Beaver tribe meet the 'World's Supreme Small Car' near the route of the Alaskan Highway. Map shows another epic journey in North America: Miss S Alexander-Sinclair completed this 10,271-mile round trip.

This very special Morris Oxford Series MO tender vehicle was built within six weeks in preparation for the rigorous 10,000-mile non-stop test of a pre-production Series II Minor saloon. The car was cradled within the articulated trailer section.

The 10,000-mile car was serviced while on the move – although not always under its own power. This was the view the service crew got from their platform at the front of the articulated trailer.

Good wishes and waves from the team supporting the Minor on its 10,000-mile reliability trial at Goodwood in October 1952.

a quagmire caused by torrential rain at Dawson Creek, British Columbia, to an all-weather gravelled surface at the $4,000,000 Peace Suspension Bridge. A new experience for the crews was the highway recipe for making tea, which necessitated putting a small packet of tea in a cup and pouring hot water on it; apparently the British method of tea infusion was unknown to the locals! That apart, one of the lasting memories of the trip was "the untiring cars that had endured so much to bring the breathtaking images of the highway to reality".

Ten thousand miles non-stop in 1952

Morris Motors Limited devised one of the Minor's most spectacular endurance feats when they planned the usual 10,000-mile test for the new Series II model powered by the Austin-developed 803cc OHV engine. Instead of the standard cumulative method of testing the car during normal working hours, they decided to make an innovative attempt to cover 10,000 miles non-stop – and to make the run serve the ends of publicity as well as those of product development and assessment.

In an aptly named booklet entitled *The Wheels Never Stopped* written by Bill Hartley, a unique story unfolds of how a four-door Morris Minor Series II saloon was adapted to enable it to complete this epic journey while at the same time allowing Morris engineers under the direction and guidance of Charles Griffin to record the vital technical information needed to enable further development work to take place.

Meticulous planning preceded this marathon event at the Goodwood racing circuit, which began at 6am on October 1st, 1952. The 24-strong team was even provided with shaving mirrors, tastefully made from car driving mirrors mounted on wooden pedestals! Sleeping and recreational facilities were provided on-site, and caterers were engaged to provide a round-the-clock service of tea, coffee, sandwiches and snacks, with main meals available to suit the duty periods. The test crews in the car carried picnic baskets with flasks of hot tea.

For publicity purposes, it was important that the car should maintain forward motion at all times, and so Morris Motors constructed a special tender from which the Minor could be serviced or repaired while on the move. This tender was an articulated vehicle based on a modified Morris half-ton van chassis, and was built over a period of six weeks. Its articulated trailer was described as resembling a two-pronged fork, built very low with the forward end stepped up to carry a collection of instruments and equipment. On each side of the prongs was a working platform some 15 inches wide, with a safety rail. Two tubular gantries were added to support the block and tackle necessary for lifting the test car one corner at a time for operations such as wheel changing.

The test car itself carried special equipment to enable the travelling observer to take the readings, and each hour he had to report from his instruments the engine coolant temperature (taken in two places), the oil temperature in the engine, gearbox and final drive, the dynamo temperature and charge rate, the engine oil level and pressure, the mileage covered and the fuel quantity remaining.

A total of six drivers shared the task of covering the 10,000 miles at an average speed of 45mph. Each was fully briefed about the procedures for servicing the vehicle in accordance with the owner's handbook, the procedure for refuelling and the procedure for entering the 'fork' of the service tender. A specially-hinged passenger seat which reclined fully eased driver changeovers at the end of each shift, and was claimed to allow driver and observer to change places without a noticeable change in lap times.

Thanks no doubt to Morris Motors' meticulous attention to detail, the whole event was a great success and attracted a lot of interest from the press, particularly during the final stages when it was also covered by TV crews. Companies associated with the manufacture and supply of parts for the Minor were quick to add

their praise and maximise their own profile – and the researchers in the Experimental Department had enough unique data to keep them usefully occupied for months.

London to Peking, 1990

Colin Moles and Michael Hoffmann completed the 1990 London to Peking Motor Challenge in a 1962 Morris Minor and in the

Colin Moles and Michael Hoffmann, pictured here at Queen's Pier, Hong Kong, visited Tiananmen Square amidst tight security as part of the 1990 London-to-Peking Motor Challenge.

The London-to-Peking Minor encountered a great variety of terrain. It is seen here negotiating its way between two large outcrops of rock in a barren desert area …

… and here in the more typically Chinese surroundings of paddy-fields. In many areas of rural China, the sight of this British classic car was a novelty unlikely to be repeated in the lifetimes of those who saw it.

process covered 9462 miles in 56 days. Setting off from Marble Arch on April 7th 1990 marked the end of a remarkable struggle to raise the £15,000 entry fee for this unique event which was based on the original concept of the Peking to Paris race first staged in 1907. Organised by the travel agency Voyages Jules Verne, the 1990 Challenge attracted a total of 65 cars, of which 15 were pre-1970 classic cars.

Just being able to participate was the fulfilment of a dream for Colin Moles, a lifelong traveller who relished the opportunity to visit different parts of the world and meet people who perhaps had never seen Europeans before – let alone a Morris Minor. The prospect of travelling across borders normally closed and entering areas previously forbidden to Westerners, as well as the challenge of travelling on unmade roads across some of the Earth's greatest deserts, had him hooked.

The car was specially prepared, its shell being expertly restored by the Morris Minor Company in Doncaster. The engine installed was a 1275cc Midget unit with a single $1^1/_2$in SU carburettor and a Metro three-branch manifold. Brakes and suspension were also uprated using Owen Burton modifications. All pipes and wiring were run inside the car, and for safety reasons a full roll cage was fitted along with two Keiper Recaro rally seats and Luke full harness seat belts. Sponsors supplied myriad other specialist parts, all designed to cope with the anticipated difficult conditions. However, the most critical addition – vital for arduous terrain – was the sump guard provided by CEF, which stretched from the front bumpers to just behind the gearbox.

The trip itself was certainly an epic journey – and for both drivers undoubtedly the trip of a lifetime. The car held up well and suffered relatively few mechanical difficulties. An oversight when fitting the clutch had costly repercussions later when it was discovered that the thrust bearing had worn through; it cost £250 to have a new one flown out to Alma Ata. Surprisingly punctures were few – only one on the whole journey. Makeshift repairs proved necessary at times too.

Colin remembers, "Just after we crossed into China, the top pipe of the radiator broke in half. For some reason it had been cut and soldered back together again previously. However, by removing the radiator cap and taping up the pipe we got through the day's drive. I found a piece of rubber hose in the car park that night and repaired it – it's still on the car today!"

Lasting impressions of the trip from both Colin and Michael relate mainly to the people and the countries visited, and of course those frightening and embarrassing moments:

"We drove between 15 miles and 470 miles per day – most of the time with either a Police or Army escort. When we left Tbilisi we lost our escort in all the traffic trying to get out of town. We knew where we were staying that night; we could read Russian and so we plotted the most direct route on the map. However, on reaching the State border the guards weren't expecting us: although our papers were in order we had obviously taken the wrong route. Eventually they gave up and let us through. We arrived safely at our hotel that night having seen large numbers of tanks and Army vehicles heading towards Baku – our next stop. We shouldn't have been there; it was the time of the military take-over of Baku. Next day we went past two scrap helicopters – well that's what we thought they were until they took off and followed us all day to make sure we didn't get lost again!

"Each day brought something new. When crossing the Gobi desert the roads were so bad we took to the desert itself and just followed the telegraph lines.

"The classic hiccough was whilst visiting the British Consulate in China. We had to drive round Tiananmen Square, a very sensitive area. The local Police and Guards were not impressed when we ran out of petrol!"

Around the world in seven years

The daunting prospect of travelling around the world in a Morris Minor is beyond most people's comprehension, but for Leeds-based Morris Minor specialist Jay Albus and his girlfriend Lynda Burke the dream became reality in January 1990 when they set out with a rough idea of their itinerary, a modicum of finance and a tremendous amount of optimism.

With a target of returning to the UK within five years, they departed with a specially-prepared Morris Minor four-door saloon emblazoned with the name of Jay's company – Major Minor Repairs Ltd of Leeds. An uneventful trip through Europe was followed by a relaxing Mediterranean cruise to Tunisia before the arduous Sahara Desert was tackled. This provided a thorough test for the car, which took something of a hammering and sustained serious damage to the rear axle, which ended up bent.

Undeterred, the pair pressed on to Kenya where they pursued the quest for a replacement axle; fortunately one turned up in a breaker's yard. After further running repairs, they pressed on to Mombasa where they made the sea crossing to the port of Bombay in India, the land of the Minor's 'Baby Hindusthan' relative.

The Morris was in good company – amongst friends – and the trips to Nepal and Kathmandu were the highlights of the expedition. Leaving India from the port of Madras, they then made their way to Australia and finally arrived in Melbourne in 1992.

At this juncture there was a significant change in the Minor's crew. Lynda Burke returned to the UK, and for a time Jay continued to tour Australia on his own. By March 1993 he had a new partner – Tania McKenna, an Australian who joined him on the flight to South America while the car made the long sea crossing to Buenos Aires. Once reunited with their Morris they set out on a major tour of South America which included a marathon trek to Tierra del Fuego. Returning northwards via Chile and Santiago, Tania – by this time eight months' pregnant – called it a day on medical advice, and reluctantly she and Jay returned home, leaving the car in Chile.

Enter Joss Browning – one-time partner with Jay and avid Morris Minor enthusiast. Determined that the trip would not fail, he took up the challenge and along with Chilean Lidia de Franchi headed to Bolivia and Colombia with the car. Here it became evident that driving to Panama was unrealistic, so yet another sea crossing was arranged from Cartagena to Panama. During 1996, Joss made his way across the border into North America via Mexico and El Paso. By the time he reached Texas, however, the engine was somewhat worse for wear. With the assistance of Moss Motors, the original engine was reconditioned and Joss headed towards Canada. Visits to the Rockies and then Niagara Falls were followed by a trip to New York for the New Year in 1997.

The final leg of this truly epic journey saw the rather tired Morris heading for Halifax, Nova Scotia, and a much deserved reception in the UK in the summer of 1997. With mission accomplished – and time to reflect – Joss is adamant that he would not undertake the trip again. Praising the Morris for its practicality and endurance he lamented the fact that perhaps understandably it needed constant attention to keep it on the road.

On a personal level, Joss recalled that his most frightening experience was waking up while sleeping in the car to find that a knife-wielding South American was stealing his trousers. He decided against protesting too much – and no, he was not wearing the trousers at the time! Nevertheless his most enduring memories are of the generosity and kindness shown to him wherever he went and of the phenomenal interest in the Morris Minor.

Jay Albus and Lynda Burke set out to go round the world in their Minor in 1990. They did not make it, but the car did – seven years later. At their send-off, National Motor Museum staff wore a variety of hats to symbolise the many countries through which the car would pass.

MINORS IN MOTOR SPORT

G.R. Holt campaigned this Series II Morris Minor in the Fourth RAC International Rally of Great Britain, and is seen here on the Ulpha stage in the Lake District.

Images of tyre-squealing Morris Minors are not the first ones to spring to mind when the subject of motor sport is under discussion. Mention the 1950s and 1960s, and household names like Stirling Moss and Graham Hill trip off the tongue. Mention the 1970s, 1980s and 1990s, and the enduring commentaries of Murray Walker invariably prompt a smile. Yet even this illustrious trio have associations with the Minor. Murray and Stirling both owned Series MM Minors and Graham tested and rallied Minors and their A35 rivals long before he got his break in Grand Prix cars.

For all its perceived limitations as a sporting car, the Morris Minor has a varied and impressive record at all levels in motor sport. Nor has it been restricted to one aspect of the sport. In rallying, circuit racing, hill-climbing, drag racing and even off-roading, the Minor has surprised many and chalked up some memorable successes. More importantly, it has enabled many drivers to experience the true thrills and spills of motor sport at club level, while allowing generations of like-minded motor sport enthusiasts to share in the excitement as spectators.

Sporting Minors in the production era

From its earliest days, the Morris Minor was entered in prestigious international rallying events. Only five months after it entered production, the Minor was competing in the 1949 Monte Carlo Rally; in the capable hands of an all-woman crew led by Mrs. E.M.

'Bill' Wisdom (wife of the well-known driver Tommy Wisdom), who was ably assisted by Betty Haig and Barbara Marshall, the Minor surpassed all expectations. Meticulous planning on the part of the crew, coupled with some impressive penalty-free driving and excellent times on the regularity sections, led to a very creditable second place in the Coupe des Dames and sixth place overall in the Under 1000cc class.

In the early 1950s, numerous crews campaigned the 918cc side-valve and the inappropriately geared 803cc OHV versions of the Minor in the Monte and in rallies in Britain which included the RAC British International Rally. Though successes were restricted to respectable class placings, the reliability of the Minor came to the fore and a great deal of pleasure was had by those hearty souls brave enough to campaign the under-powered Minor in almost standard specification against much more powerful and more obviously sporting machinery.

Recollections of those who managed to finish such events invariably give rise to the view that it was the taking part rather than the winning which was important. Not that this stopped them from pushing themselves and their cars to the limit. In 1953, an all-Irish crew of Ray Noble, Roland Graham and Garnett Wolseley gained a finisher's award on the Monte after a particularly snowy and gruelling event – a fact reinforced by the loss of life sustained when the crew of a MkVII Jaguar crashed out. The Minor, supplied ex-works on a sale or return basis (something which would never have happened in later years!) did not quite fit the bill. Although a two-door saloon was requested, a heavier four-door was supplied. Modifications were minimal: Brittain's, the Dublin assemblers of Morris Minors, fitted sump shields and added stronger valve springs to the engine, Lucas improved the lighting with the addition of spotlights and fog lamps, but the only other modification seems to have been the fitting of a map holder!

The camaraderie was Ray Noble's lasting impression of the event. As for the Minor, he lamented its lack of power and the inadequacies of its brakes. He recalled illustrious names including Sydney Allard, Stirling Moss and Raymond Baxter, and the garden party hosted by Prince Rainier. He also recalled his lucky escape in not catching the scheduled ship to Ireland; the Minor was booked on the *Victoria* which went down on that sailing.

Pat Moss did much to restore the reputation of the Morris Minor in both national and international rallies. The 948cc A-series engine which became available in the Minor 1000 in 1956 was much more receptive to tuning than earlier Minor engines, and provided the vital ingredient required to make the Minor at least competitive. With the gutsy Pat at the wheel, it was certainly that! Amongst the fleet of competition cars at the BMC Competitions Department, a couple of Minor saloons received the works treatment. Under the watchful eye of Marcus Chambers, Competitions Manager, Nobby Hall prepared a grey four-door registered NJB 277 and a green two-door registered NMO 933.

Ray Brookes drove the works Minor 1000 NJB 277 in the 1957 Sestrière Rally, and finished a creditable third in class. Pat Moss campaigned the same car in the Tulip Rally, and in exceptionally cold and snowy conditions finished 16th in class and 90th overall. In the same event, John Gott and Chris Tooley piloted NMO 933, but they fared no better, finishing 108th overall.

Soon after this event an interesting change occurred: Pat Moss switched cars and NMO 933 switched colours. As a result of over-exuberence on the part of one of the apprentices, NMO required some major structural repairs, and Pat's unusual superstition about green cars no doubt influenced the decision to repaint the car white. In its new livery, 'Granny' (as NMO 933 was dubbed by Pat) was to achieve major success in her hands.

In the tough Liège-Rome-Liège rally, the Minor struggled through to a creditable second place in the Coupe des Dames in spite of damper trouble and the loss of a gearbox drain plug. This achievement was all the more impressive when the Minor was

An all-Irish crew led by Ray Noble collected a finisher's award in the 1953 Monte Carlo Rally, in this Irish-registered four-door saloon supplied by the factory.

The Minor's superior road-holding and handling made it a popular choice for amateur motor sport enthusiasts. Here, three Irish-registered Minors line up in preparation for a local event in County Monaghan.

Pat Moss gave the Minor credibility as a rally car by her exploits with this example, NMO 933, affectionately known as 'Granny'. She is pictured with Ann Wisdom on the 1957 Liège-Rome-Liège Rally, on her way to 23rd place overall and second place in the Coupe des Dames.

'Granny' gets off to a flier at Crystal Palace on one of the special stages of the RAC Rally. Pat Moss declined to purchase the car in 1960 when it was offered to her by the factory for £500.

Harry Sutcliffe and Mrs P. Sutcliffe rallied this specially-equipped Minor (near right) in the 1954 Monte Carlo event, starting in Athens and finishing 295th overall. Despite problems with axle tramp, many enthusiastic motor sport competitors raced Morris Minors with varying degrees of success, and here (far right) a Minor is being put through its paces at Goodwood in 1956.

declared the smallest car ever to finish the Liège; and to it could be added fourth place in its class and 23rd place overall. Pat continued to rally the Minor in both national and international events, but the only other notable success was in the RAC British International Rally where in 1958 she finished fourth overall and took the Ladies' prize. In this event she was ably supported by W. H. Wadham, also in a Morris Minor 1000, who finished fifth overall out of a total of 196 starters.

Tweaks to the rally cars were kept to a minimum. Writing in *Sporting Cars* magazine in 1984 about his venture in NMO 933 with

John Gott on the Tulip Rally, Chris Tooley recalled that the Abingdon mechanics' wizardry extended only to adding stronger valve springs, a larger carburettor, an oil cooler and front brakes from the Wolseley 1500 – not a massive array of extras!

However, those more inclined to circuit racing, where outright straight-line speed had greater importance, did seek to modify the cars within what now look like rather loosely drafted regulations. Most of the modifications sought to overcome some of the Minor's inherent weaknesses, in particular a lack of power, inadequate braking and the infamous axle tramp.

The Minor was unquestionably a popular choice of car within the racing fraternity. Although handicapped by its weight (it was 1½cwt heavier than its A30 and later A35 stablemates from BMC), its superior roadholding and cornering ability brought some compensation. Coupled with the fact that it was cheap to buy and easy to work on, this endeared it to many. At club level, of course, standard road-going Minors were commonplace in rallies and on the circuits. More serious competitors adopted various modifications, depending on the event being tackled. Typical of the competitors who enjoyed their racing to the full are Pat Kennett and Allan Staniforth, both of whom competed extensively in their Minors in the mid-1950s before progressing to more powerful and sophisticated machinery

Pat Kennett's multi-faceted approach was typical of an era when it was possible to use the same car in a wide range of events. His white tourer was a familiar sight in motor sport events in Northern England between 1956 and 1958, and was equally at home competing in speed hill-climbs at Barbon, Mancetter, Harewood and Catterick, circuit races at Oulton Park and Silverstone, rallies in Wales, the Lake District and Yorkshire, and sprints at Rhyddymwyn, New Brighton and Oulton Park.

Initially, the Kennett Minor was run with twin SU carburettors and a raised compression ratio. Morris Cowley front torsion bars and front brakes improved handling appreciably while a pair of radius rods beneath the rear springs helped reduce axle tramp. However, the car ran a variety of engines, chosen to suit the power output required for different events. For sprint and hill-climb events, the Minor had a special engine with a Wade supercharger to

Allan Staniforth's Alta-headed Tourer is seen cornering hard on its first outing – the Morecambe International Rally of May 1956. A split second after this picture was taken during the promenade tests, the car nearly demolished a section of iron railings! As this was a road event, bumpers and spotlights were retained on the car, which also sported a home-made twin exhaust, visible below the passenger door.

boost its mid-speed output. However, as top speed was lower with the supercharger than it was with twin SUs and natural aspiration, two competition engines, both fully balanced by Laystall, were used for circuit racing and rallying.

Modest results accrued and the occasional class win in rallying events was recorded. However, even though engine changes could be done in half an hour (which should give modern enthusiasts food for thought!), the sheer effort involved in repeatedly doing so eventually ended the Minor's involvement in competitions. Pat Kennett's recollections of his involvement with the Minor are favourable. He says of his years competing with the Minor, "I had an enormous amount of fun with that car. Indeed it was probably more fun for my money than anything else I used in competitions in a

THE WORKS-PREPARED MINORS AND THEIR RESULTS

Date	Event	Car	Registration	Rally no	Crew	Result
2/57	Sestrières	Minor 1000	NJB 277		R Brookes/E Brookes	3rd in class
5/57	Tulip	Minor 1000	NMO 933	161	John Gott/Chris Tooley	108th overall, 12th in class
5/57	Tulip	Minor 1000	NJB 277		Pat Moss/Ann Wisdom	90th overall, 16th in class
8/57	Liège-Rome-Liège	Minor 1000	NMO 933	39	Pat Moss/Ann Wisdom	23rd overall, 4th in class, 2nd Ladies
1/58	Monte Carlo	Minor 1000	NMO 933	313	Pat Moss/Ann Wisdom	Retired after accident
3/58	RAC Rally	Minor 1000	NMO 933	201	Pat Moss/Ann Wisdom	4th overall, 1st in class, 1st Ladies
9/58	Viking	Minor 1000	NMO 933		Pat Moss/ Ann Wisdom	4th in class, 2nd Ladies
3/59	Circuit of Ireland	Minor 1000	NMO 933	1	Pat Moss/Ann Wisdom	14th overall, 2nd in class, 1st Ladies
11/59	RAC Rally	Minor 1000	NMO 933	121	Pat Moss/Ann Wisdom	26th overall, 3rd Ladies

Views of Allan Staniforth's Tourer. Fabricated alloy dash has additional gauges and large rev counter. The speedometer was ahead of the passenger, flanked by a clock; above them is a cowled map-reading lamp. Note the electric demisting bar attached to the windscreen with suction feet, and the special heater in the passenger footwell, with ducting to the driver's accelerator foot. Attached to the passenger's door handle is a scrutineer's ticket. Engine shots show Alta OHV conversion, complete with home-made inlet manifold. The carburettors were 1¹/₈in SUs, and a four-branch exhaust was fitted. There was space for a cold air box, not fitted in this 1957 photograph, and the standard oil filler was replaced by the much larger lidded type from a Ford 10, visible at lower left.

strictly amateur motor sport career which spanned 45 years. Above all, it was absolutely safe. Once we had Cowley front brakes, the Minor's exceptional basic stability kept it out of trouble, no matter what abuses it was required to accept".

Allan Staniforth, a canny northerner and former *Daily Mirror* reporter, fulfilled his ambition to go motor racing when he acquired a side-valve Morris Minor Tourer in 1956. First impressions were not favourable: "Looking back, I remember the painful shock I got when I drove NKA 266 for the first time just before buying it. It was gutless beyond belief, the nice gearbox having to be operated like an Olympic fencer's foil to keep the car moving". The addition of an Alta OHV conversion transformed the car, though, and with the added stopping power afforded by Mintex M16 shoes on the front and M11s on the back plus special clutch linings, the car was set for its foray into competition.

Like many of his contemporaries, Allan was frustrated by the axle tramp – the Minor's Achilles heel. He described this graphically in one of his motor racing reports as "the bugbear of every competitive Minor owner from Goodwood to California – appalling rear axle bounce and tramp at the most embarrassing moments". He went on, "For those who have not experienced it – on trying to leave the line in a driving test race or hill climb, the whole axle leaps up and down vertically while the car isn't going anywhere because the wheels aren't touching the ground long enough to send it on its way. Lifting off stops the bounce but the car

has more than enough power to start it again on accelerating and even in changing into second. When they think of the whole seconds, let alone tenths going to waste while this is happening, strong motoring men are near to tears".

To improve weight distribution, Allan moved the battery of his car to a recess cut into its floor, and, despite the handicap of axle tramp, he went on to race his Minor successfully in the 1956-57 seasons. Outings to Catterick, Croft and Sherburn in Elmet, plus a 750 Motor Club Relay at Silverstone, proved instructive and early success came at Croft with a class win in the Up To 1000cc Class. The full results of that event reveal that the Minor had beaten 32 other vehicles, including those in classes for vehicles up to 2600cc.

Success continued in 1958 with no fewer than five class wins, a high-speed trial award and a win in the Aston Martin Owners Club 'David Brown' Relay Race, which involved teams of three cars. The Alta-powered Minor even set some course records. Though he progressed to racing a Rochdale GT glass fibre Special and enjoyed a successful and varied motoring career, Allan recalls with affection his days with the Minor and remembers only too well that everything did not go according to plan. "I remember fitting some rear remoulds with coiled wire in the treads which theoretically wore down into little wire spikes. Dramatic contemporary adverts showed tiger's claws gripping the road. Suitably impressed, I went out of Silverstone pits on them first time and straight off backwards at Copse!"

Many other drivers took to the Minor and raced with varying degrees of success against A35s, DKWs and Renault Dauphines. Prominent drivers included Alan Foster, who raced various Minors including an early Alta-headed saloon and later a 'semi-works' Morris 1000 following his involvement with MG in BMC's Competitions Department. Then there was Harry Ratcliffe, whose exploits made him a popular figure, particularly on northern circuits, and F. G. Marriott, who gave the A35 drivers a run for their money in his Minor 1000 but invariably ended up coming off second best.

If straight-line speed was not the Minor's forte, then endurance racing was and the car chalked up some notable achievements overseas. Some of the most striking were the early successes in the 1950s at Sebring in Florida. In the 1950 six-hour Grand Prix at Endurance, Bob Gegen finished 14th overall while Monty Thomas took his car to 17th place. In 1952, in the First Annual 12-hours at Sebring, Roger Wing and Steven Spitler drove their Series MM to a very creditable 15th place out of 32 finishers. The following year they finished 31st out of 51, and in the process they left in their wake much more prestigious metal in the form of Jaguar XK120s, two Ferrari 225Ss, an Aston Martin DB3 and a Maserati A6GCS. Other overseas achievements included a win for an enterprising Tasmanian, H. C. Hawthorne, who took the honours in the Up To 1100cc Class in the 1957 Mobilgas Around Australia Rally.

David Burrows chalked up some notable successes in the Pre-1957 Historic Saloon Championship, winning both Class D and the overall title in 1979.

Sporting Minors in the post-production era

So far as motor sport was concerned, the heyday of the Morris Minor was most certainly the 1950s. Although Minor production continued until 1971, motor sport enthusiasts in the UK showed little interest in the car which was by this time outmoded as a serious contender. However, interest in the Minor was re-awakened in the 1980s with the establishment of a series of nostalgic motor sport activities. The emergence of Historic Saloon Car racing and Historic Rallying rekindled interest in those cars which were emerging as classics, and once again the Minor was in the spotlight.

An early competitor in the Pre-57 Historic Saloon Car Club Championship was David Burrows. In 1979 he purchased a 1957 four-door saloon for £30; £1000 later he had a race-prepared car fitted with all the permitted modifications. The vehicle had to be road legal and was required to be driven to the circuit. Competing in Class D, which allowed for larger front brake drums, a servo and slightly wider wheels, Burrows put together an impressive string of class wins and fastest laps which culminated in the Class D Championship but more importantly the 1979 Pre-57 Classic Saloon Car Club Championship.

A temporary diversion the following season led to further success with a MG Magnette, but 1981 saw Burrows return to a Morris Minor and entry in Class D of the Pre-57 Classic Saloon Car Club Championship. Impressive driving once again secured an Overall Class win and led to a drive in a Mk1 Jaguar the following season and a second Overall Championship win.

In the 1982 and 1983 seasons, Patrick McCloy and Peter Hannaway took up the challenge, but were not as competitive in their Minor. However, the appearance of Robin Moore in 1987 restored the Minor's fortunes. In an extremely successful four-year period, he took his modified Minor to three Class Championship wins for 1987, 1989 and 1990 in the Up To 1250cc Roadgoing Class, and clocked up no fewer than seven lap records, all at different race circuits.

Much of the interest in motor sport in the Minor's post-

Steve Jenner took to historic racing between 1989 and 1991, and in his best season finished runner-up in the Modified Class.

Morris Minor specialist Jim Funnell has competed regularly in the Silhouette series. His GRP-bodied, space-framed car is powered by a 1300cc Ford Cosworth engine which gives it a top speed of 116mph.

Dedicated competitors in hill-climbing and drag racing at least remained loyal to the Minor bodyshell while they sought to extract the maximum power and acceleration. The best-known exponent of the Minor in this branch of motor sport was Nic Mann, whose car received worldwide acclaim. Built as a hill-climb racer, his Rover V8-powered Minor was always kept street legal and was driven to and from events, which Nic claimed was as enjoyable as the racing itself. He regularly put some 4000 miles a year on the odometer.

Autocar magazine tested the car twice and produced some staggering results. In October 1980 it was heralded as "by far the fastest road legal car to 100mph" that the magazine had tested. When retested in November 1981 it was even quicker. With nitrous oxide injection added to the turbocharged Rover 3.5-litre V8 engine, a time of 11.8 seconds was recorded for the standing quarter-mile. Impressive acceleration giving 0-60mph in 3.4 seconds and 0-100mph in 7.9 seconds underlined the uniqueness of Mann's Minor. The significance of these times is put in perspective when they are compared with those achieved by Jaguar's XJ220 supercar: *Autocar's* figures for the Jaguar closely matched those it had recorded for the Minor eleven years earlier! Meanwhile,

production era has focused on modified cars. Serious contenders in the Silhouette Racing Series included Leicestershire-based Jim Funnell, whose Minor creations paid lip service to the original marque. However, his space-framed cars which sported high-performance engines, such as fuel-injected Ford Cosworth 1300cc units, owed little to the original Minor. His 1994 mount stood a mere 49in high, but was capable of 116mph.

With acceleration times of 0-130mph in 11.1 seconds, it is hard to believe that this ultra-quick Minor (far left) owned by Nic Mann was street legal. The basis of its engine was a 3.5-litre Rover V8. Fitted with big, fire-breathing American V8s (near left), Minors are very popular with Scandinavian drag racers who enjoy some wild rides thanks to the short wheelbase.

Drag racing is a popular aspect of motor sport among younger Minor owners. This purpose-built dragster pick-up built by Robin Moore, Colin Moore and Bob Roberts is extensively modified from standard.

development work had continued on the car and by the time *Street Machine* magazine tested it in 1995, barely credible figures of 11.1 seconds for 0-130mph and a maximum speed of 150mph were being produced. Not surprisingly, *Street Machine* readers were impressed and voted it '*Street Machine* Feature Car of the Year, 1995'.

As well as clocking up many successes on the hill-climb scene, Nic Mann's Minor took on and beat mighty American-engined machines on the drag strip. In 1982, 1983, 1984, 1986 and 1991, his car secured an unmatched five victories in the prestigious Annual

Street Racer Championship run for street legal cars over a standing quarter-mile at York Dragway. The last victory was in the hands of the car's new owner Bill Sherratt, who acquired the car after new hill-climb regulations rendered it uncompetitive. By any standards the car has had a glittering career considering that Nic's mother used to go shopping in it!

Morris Minors have continued to be a popular choice for drag racing. American V8-powered Minors have entertained on drag strips in Scandinavia, while in the UK Phil Drewitt has sought to

The Morris Minor once owned by the Archbishop of Canterbury exceeded all expectations when it finished 14th overall in the 1981 Himalayan Rally. In the capable hands of Philip Young and the Rev. Rupert Jones, the car overcame all obstacles to record a memorable result against much more modern machinery.

This action picture taken on the 1985 Coronation Rally staged by the Welsh Counties Motor Club shows the author competing in a Derrington-powered 1950 Series MM.

emulate Nic Mann's achievements with his 'Green Monster'. Interest remains high in this aspect of motor sport and competition looks set to scale new heights with Minors such as the Moore/Roberts Wade-supercharged, 150bhp Dragster pick-up which took to the strip in 1997, and Jaguar V12-powered Minors being developed.

Rallying also received a boost in the post-production era. An audacious attempt by Philip Young, former editor of *Sporting Cars* magazine, to compete in the 1981 Himalayan Rally in a Morris Minor provided the springboard for a revival in Historic Rallying. Young teamed up with the Rev. Rupert Jones – affectionately known as the Rallying Vicar – and appropriately acquired the then Archbishop of Canterbury's Morris Minor, which was a perfect, low-mileage four-door saloon.

Preparations to transform this former cleric's carriage into a competition rally car were thorough, and an interesting link with the former BMC Competitions Department and the Pat Moss rally car was established when ace mechanic Nobby Hall was engaged to do the engine preparation. The original 1098cc engine was replaced by a 1275cc Midget unit which was mildly tuned. In 1982, Philip Young noted in correspondence with the author that,

"The chassis was standard as far as any strengthening was concerned apart from the 'skidding' of the rear spring hangers and the fitting of a sump shield. Extra instruments included a dual water temperature/oil pressure gauge given by Abingdon. This was in fact an MGB instrument, taken out of the dash of a works TR7 driven by Timo Makinen in the Thousand Lakes Rally. A second-hand pair of ex-Tony Pond seat belts were also scrounged.

"The car could do a ton on the standard axle ratio, the close ratio gears were super, and we caned it non-stop. It handled very well indeed thanks to its 165 x 14 Avon Arctic Steels. All things considered it did very well bearing in mind it started in 67th place and rose to ninth, overtaking more cars than anyone else to win the small car class. I put it all down to the agile nature of the Minor and the truly unburstable feel of the A-Series engine. Chris Bruce, a long distance rally driver of Escorts, was the one-man service manager who undertook final preparation of the car. He was pretty impressed and reckoned that it would be possible to build a truly demon Morris Minor capable of achieving results. He had to re-build the front suspension after a jungle section and the fact that the car did so well is largely due to his untiring efforts in keeping her nailed together.

"Rev. Rupert Jones was a noted driver and set international long distance records in Austin A35s. He also rallied the Minor's big brother, the Riley One-Point-Five, as well as Austin Healey 3000s. On the Himalayan, he didn't make one mistake with the maps and showed remarkable stamina, particularly at the end, when he drove the car out of the mountains through the night to Delhi while I slept – a remarkable feat as he had been awake just as long as I had. He drove the last stage when the brakes failed and slid the car up a dry stone wall to slow her down!".

Sadly the Rev. Rupert Jones is no longer with us, but Philip Young remains intensely proud of their achievement in finishing 14th overall in the toughest rally in the world – beating many more modern works-prepared cars in the process and winning the small car category. The car itself now resides in a motor museum in New Zealand. As for Philip Young, he has worked tirelessly to promote Historic Rallying and provide opportunities for others to participate in Historic Motor Sport events. In addition, the Historic Rally Car Register has actively promoted many domestic events in the UK such as the Welsh Counties Coronation Rally, and supports events

for Historic Rally cars in conjunction with the prestigious RAC International Rally. However, the annual Monte Carlo Challenge has emerged as one of the most popular events and Morris Minors continue to be represented on the list of starters!

Opportunities still abound for active involvement in motor sport and the Morris Minor is still capable of springing a few surprises, just as it did in the good old days. Competition is not only confined to the UK. In the USA the success of Morris Minors at Sebring was celebrated with a flourish in 1995 with a special reunion organised by the Sportscar Vintage Racing Association. Tom Cotter, who regularly races his 1957 Minor in SVRA events, led the way racing a Minor at the famous Florida circuit for the first time since 1953.

Historic racing is also popular in America, and Tom Cotter races this modified Minor in Sportscar Vintage Racing Association events. The car was pictured here at Sebring in Florida, evoking memories of the Minor's success in endurance events of the 1950s feats recalled at a special reunion meeting held in 1995.

The engine of the Moore/Roberts dragster is a BMC A-plus type, fitted with a Wade RO20 supercharger and water/methanol injection. It can put out 150bhp.

MODIFYING THE MINOR

The Alta overhead-valve conversion was marketed by Geoffrey Taylor of the Alta Car and Engineering Company Ltd in Surbiton, Surrey. This head was cast in Birmidal aluminium alloy, and had hardened Brico valve seats.

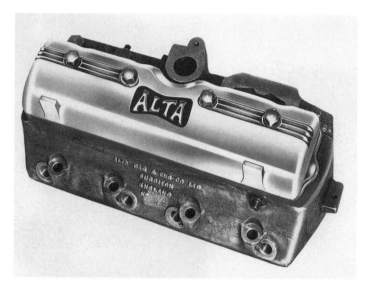

For all its many virtues, the Morris Minor did not satisfy everybody. The main source of dissatisfaction right from the beginning was that its performance did not live up to the promise so tantalisingly held out by its handling, and from the very early days it received the attentions of the go-faster brigade.

Some early conversions

During the early 1950s, the British motoring press reported on at least two engine transplants which were intended to give the Minor additional performance. However, neither of these brave one-off conversions seems to have inspired imitators, and the complex engineering which they needed makes them appear bizarre to modern eyes.

Autosport reported during 1953 on the transplant into a 1949 Series MM of a mildly tuned 1172cc engine from a Ford Prefect. Acceleration through the gears was improved and less gear changing was needed overall, while the top speed increased to over 70mph. However, the overall result was at best only satisfactory, and the Ford engine proved to be less smooth than the original Morris side-valve.

Two years later, *The Autocar* reported comprehensively on a 'Surprise Package' when they road-tested a Series II Tourer fitted with a 1200cc Austin A40 engine and gearbox. The engine had an A40 Sports cylinder head, twin SU carburettors and double valve springs, and powered the car to a genuine 80mph, but it shook violently whenever a first-gear start was attempted. *The Autocar* concluded that the cost of the conversion was in any case too great to be commercially viable.

Bolt-on engine conversions

It is no surprise that bolt-on conversions of the existing engine proved more practical and popular than major conversions like

In 1954, the Alta conversion cost £48 10s 0d. It transformed the performance of the standard side-valve engine, increasing top speed to 80mph.

these. As many Minor owners felt the need for additional speed, a number of options were made available.

One of the most straightforward modifications was marketed by V.W. Derrington, a well-known and highly respected purveyor of speed equipment, which had the distinction of listing Stirling Moss among its clientele. *Motor Sport* in 1952 tested a Series MM two-door Saloon registered MMM 398 and concurred with Stirling's preference for the Morris Minor; he owned a similar car, MMM 771, and had 'souped it up' using Derrington equipment.

The modifications which could be carried out in stages involved fitting double valve springs to reduce valve bounce. Terry inner springs were used in conjunction with standard outer ones. At the same time more durable Valkrom exhaust valves were fitted.

Then followed the distinctive Derrington 'Silvertop' aluminium cylinder head which raised the compression ratio to 7.2:1 from 6.5:1. Finally, harder Champion L10S sparking plugs were added.

Derrington's package also offered the option of a Lucas Sports coil, a 'deep-note' exhaust system which reduced back pressure, and twin carburettors on an adapted version of the inlet manifold. To add to the modified car's image, if not its performance, customers could add a Derrington Sports Steering Wheel and a specially designed Derrington Gear Lever Extension.

The results of the Derrington conversion were impressive and *Motor Sport's* findings were endorsed by Wilson McComb when he tested a similarly converted 1952 Series MM Tourer for *Autosport* a year later.

V.W. Derrington's Silvertop cylinder head significantly improved acceleration and top speed when fitted along with double valve springs, twin carburettors and a deep-note exhaust system.

One of the most unusual and rare conversions is this Australian one, which turned the side-valve engine into an overhead-valve type. It was produced by Mazengarb in Sydney, and matched the performance of British-made conversions although its configuration was distinctly different.

The ultimate period 'mod' for the redoubtable side-valve engine was marketed by the Alta Car and Engineering Co. Ltd., based in Kingston, Surrey, England. It involved a conversion from side valves to overhead valves and at the 1955 price of £45 complete plus a fitting charge of £4 it represented good value.

The cylinder head was cast in Birmidal aluminium and carried a line of inclined overhead valves with dual springs. These were operated by pushrods and forged rockers from the tappets of the original side-valve engine. Brico valve seats were inserted and the inlet valve diameter was increased by 2mm. Designed with siamesed inlet ports, the cylinder head had the advantage of being able to use the existing inlet and exhaust manifolds without any modification. However, a short exhaust pipe extension was needed and a different jet needle was required for the standard H1 SU carburettor. No meaningful advantage was apparent if twin carburettors were used.

Greatly improved acceleration through the gears and a maximum speed in the region of 75mph ensured that road testers in the 1950s were mightily impressed with the Alta conversion. However, even Geoffrey Taylor, who masterminded this innovation, would have been incredulous if he had been told that Alta-headed Minors would still be able to hold their own 40 years later, in the traffic conditions of the 1990s!

These tuning developments in the UK were paralleled to an uncanny degree in Australia, one of the largest export markets for the early Morris Minor models. The Melbourne-based Monaro Motors devised and marketed an add-on twin-carburettor set-up which markedly improved performance. Unlike the UK versions which retained the existing inlet manifold, the 'Aussie' version used two special short cast bronze manifolds and a thin 3/4in balance tube with an MG linkage assembly. To complete the package, the fitting of a special Burgess type silencer with a 3/16in oversized tailpipe was recommended – an addition Monaro Motors claimed would limit burn-out on the number one exhaust valve. The resulting improvements in performance mirrored those of similar UK twin-carburettor conversions.

There was a side-valve to overhead-valve conversion available in Australia, too, and this offered similar performance gains to the Alta conversion. Developed by the Gear Manufacturing Co. Pty. Ltd., at St. Mary's, New South Wales, the Australian OHV conversion was marketed under the name of its designer, A.J. Mazengarb. In terms of its layout, however, it was startlingly different to the Alta conversion, switching the carburettor, manifold and radiator hose and header tank connection to the off-side while the dynamo was moved to the near-side. Further changes for the Mazengarb overhead-valve conversion included Australian-made items such as a sports coil, duplex valve springs, AC 10mm spark plugs and revised exhaust.

Back in the UK even more strenuous efforts were being made to extract the last ounce of power from the 918cc side-valve engine. Supercharging had once been thought of as the domain of the motor racing fraternity, but it was now being promoted as an alternative means of increasing performance for the ordinary Minor owner. A number of superchargers could be bought for around £80, those by Shorrocks and Marshall Nordec being the most popular. The practicality of fitting a 'blower' was stressed in contemporary reports in *The Autocar* and *The Motor*, and though tests showed some increase in fuel consumption, the benefits were considered to far outweigh this small inconvenience.

Superchargers remained a recommended way of improving the Minor's performance long after the demise of the original side-valve engine, and right through into the era of the A-series engine which began in 1952. This engine provided greater scope for tuning, and a number of well-established reputable companies offered single and twin-carburettor conversions and additional modifications

CONVERSIONS ARE AVAILABLE FOR

Austin A.30 A.35 A.40 A.50
  A.55 A.90 (Six)

New Ford Anglia. Prefect.

Ford Consul 1 and 2.
Ford Zephyr 1 and 2.
Ford Zodiac.

M.G. Magnette (ZA) (ZB)
  1¼-litre Y-type.
  1250c.c. XPAG Type TB
  TC TD TF.
  1500c.c. XPEG Type TF

Morris Minor s.v. and o.h.v.
  Series II and 1000.
Morris Cowley
Morris Oxford Series II and
  III.
Morris Isis

Nash Metropolitan and Austin
  Metropolitan.

Standard 8 and 10.

Wolseley 4/44.
Wolseley 15/50.

Hillman Minx Series I and II
Sunbeam Rapier.
Renault Dauphine.
Vauxhall Victor.

Alexander offered a range of conversion options to improve performance. Though rarely seen on Minors today, they proved popular contemporary modifications and were often seen on competition cars.

ALEXANDER CONVERSIONS

providing different stages of tune up to and including race and rally specifications. Among these companies were Alexander Engineering based at Haddenham, Buckinghamshire, and Powerplus at the Wycliffe Motor Co. Ltd. in Stroud, Gloucestershire. Under the direction of international rally driver John Sprinzel and Graham Hill, later to be a Formula 1 World Champion, Speedwell Performance Conversions in London also provided ultra-quick Minors, as well as A30s and A35s which more than held their own in competitive events.

Working to the same basic formula, the conversions by Alexander, Speedwell and Powerplus certainly pepped up the overall performance, although there was a cost in terms of petrol consumption. However, the emphasis remained on engine modification and carburation, and little or nothing was offered to improve stopping power because the Minor's brakes were considered to be adequate!

For an all-inclusive price of £44 in 1958, Alexander Engineering modified the cylinder head by reshaping and polishing the combustion chambers and ports, and in the process raised the compression to 8.9:1. Special valve springs were fitted to raise the speed at which the valves started to bounce, and a cast light alloy induction manifold with an integral balance pipe was installed along with twin 1¹/₈in SU carburettors, each with its own air filter. A special feature was the new elbow outlet bolted to the centre exhaust port, which discharged gases direct into the top of the existing hot spot chamber and gave a much improved flow.

Powerplus treated the cylinder head in much the same way to produce a compression ratio of 8.75:1. It was supplied on an exchange basis for £67 17s 6d, and came with twin 20-degree semi-downdraught SU carburettors, a Burgess type straight-through silencer with a three-branch exhaust manifold and a recalibrated speedometer. The Powerplus system allowed for outstanding

improvements in both acceleration and maximum speed – which was claimed to be 75mph.

Speedwell Performance Conversions offered a package which promised a power output in excess of 50bhp. The cylinder head was remachined to match a master head which had been flow-tested. Combustion chamber contours and ports were reshaped, and inlet valves of improved shape and exhaust valves in better-quality steel were fitted together with special springs. Like Alexander and Powerplus, Speedwell fitted twin SU carburettors. For an additional £1 10s 0d, a silicon-damped 110mph speedometer could also be supplied on an exchange basis.

The accepted engine transplants

Although a vast array of engines have found their way into Minors over the years, from Mazda rotaries to 7.5-litre Chevrolet V8s, a few conversions have been popular enough to become regarded as accepted practice. All of them fit in with the Minor's awkward bulkhead-mounted steering rack, which is the main obstacle facing any proposed engine transplant.

Riley 1.5-litre engine

The quest for enjoying more power in a Minor through cubic capacity rather than tuning inevitably led pioneers in the direction of the Minor's big brother, the Riley One-Point-Five. An unstressed 68bhp from the twin-carburettor B-series engine certainly made sense, and fitting was not that difficult, but there were snags.

The biggest problem was the length of the engine. With the rearward positioning dictated by the cut-out in the Riley's gearbox bellhousing to clear the steering rack, the front of the engine and the radiator wanted to occupy the same space. With no room to reposition the radiator, the most common solution was to remove the centre cores from it to clear the water pump pulley. Understandably, this made cooling efficiency marginal. The B-series is also no lightweight, and its extra mass negated most improvements that would have been gained from fitting uprated suspension and wider wheels.

It was still a very popular swap, though, because it involved very little fabrication and all donor parts could be obtained from one car. The Riley's propshaft would fit with the addition of a small spacer, its hydraulic clutch master cylinder was easy to adapt with a simple bracket, and the bigger front brakes and taller-geared

V8 engines regularly find their way into more radically modified Minors with separate chassis and different suspension layouts. These two are a 3.5-litre Rover in Steve Uragello's pick-up and a 5-litre Ford in Nic Cook's two-door saloon.

differential were bolt-on jobs. In theory the single-carburettor engine from the Riley's brother, the Wolseley 1500, could be used just as easily, although there was little point as it had just 50bhp.

MG Midget 1275cc engine

The most popular engine swap for Minors came from a logical development by BMC themselves. Introduced in 1964 in transverse form for the Mini Cooper, the ultimate development of the A-series engine found its way into the Mk III MG Midget in 1966. Adapted as it was to mate to many of the parts the Midget shared with the Minor, it was the closest thing there was to a straight swap. With 65bhp on offer and no weight penalty, these engines started turning up in Minors as soon as they became available from crashed MGs in the late 1960s. Certainly the swap was being freely talked about in *Hot Car* magazine by 1969, and the 1275cc A-series in one form or another is still the most popular engine transplant today.

The Midget engine is best accompanied by its matching (stronger) gearbox. It can also be used with the gearbox from a 1098cc Minor, but unless fully rebuilt this cannot be expected to last long in the hands of an enthusiastic driver. What the Midget does bring with it is a tougher, diaphragm spring clutch in place of the Minor's coil-sprung one. In the Midget, however, the clutch is operated by hydraulics. The slave cylinder can be removed and the Minor's mechanical clutch rod can be fitted to the Midget's release fork, but this leaves the pedal feeling rather heavy and with a short travel. Many owners are happy to live with this, but the best option is to fit a hydraulic master cylinder, as with the Riley engine.

The engine steady bracket that attaches to the cylinder head needs a V-notch cut into it to accommodate the different angle of the heater outlet studs, and the fan blades need careful adjusting to clear the crankcase breather. In addition, a decision has to be made about the exhaust manifold, and the choice rests between a tubular aftermarket type and one from a later A-series engine.

Marina 1275cc engine

Although in essence the same engine as used in the Midget, the 1275cc A-series used in the Morris Marina or the later Ital has enough fundamental differences to make it far from an easy bolt-in swap. It also has only 60bhp in standard form, making it less attractive than the Midget. However, when increased interest in classic cars caused supplies of homeless Midget engines to dry up by the early 1980s, the ever-increasing numbers of Marinas in

This 1275cc Marina engine is fitted to a standard Minor formerly owned by Amanda Hazlett (née Wright).

scrapyards started to look attractive to owners of Minors.

Most incompatibility with the Minor stems from British Leyland's use of an all-synchromesh four-speed Triumph-based gearbox in the Marina. Two options present themselves, although as neither is that simple the choice comes down to individual preference and budget. The cheaper way is to keep the Minor gearbox. To do this, the Minor flywheel has to be re-drilled to the six-bolt fixing on the Marina crank and fitted with a special centre spigot. The Minor's engine backplate also has to be modified to fit the 1275 engine. If power increases are envisaged it is also worth converting to a diaphragm clutch. Several specialists will provide these items on an exchange basis.

If the Marina gearbox is to be fitted, one-inch shorter front engine mounting towers are needed to allow the clutch slave cylinder to clear the steering rack. Obviously this also demands a conversion to hydraulic clutch operation. A new engine backplate is required to reposition the starter motor, which would otherwise foul the chassis rail. The Minor front engine plate is also required and fits straight on, but the gearbox crossmember has to be repositioned and it is also necessary to fit a new propshaft.

Ford V4 engine

Ford's V4 was a fairly popular choice among those who customised Minors in the 1970s and early 1980s, if only for the reason that in

Ford's 2-litre V4 fitted without any cutting and was popular because of its large capacity, but its extra weight unbalanced the handling. This example was pictured in Nick Diss's two-door saloon.

The Fiat twin-cam fits very well and carries no weight penalty, despite capacities up to 2-litres. The tidy installation here is by Robin Beardmore.

2-litre form it was the largest capacity engine that could be fitted without cutting the car about or changing the front suspension. Run with twin exhaust pipes, it also made a decent noise and – on paper at least – 102bhp sounded an attractive proposition.

In reality, the V4 is an extremely heavy lump of iron which puts too much weight too far forward and adversely affects the car's handling. It also has a number of well-known shortcomings, being slow to rev and prone to vibration and blown head gaskets. In its favour is the fact that it fits as if made for the job. New engine mounts and gearbox crossmember are simple fabrications, and an exhaust system can be made by cutting and re-welding the tubular headers from a V4 Capri and adapting the rest of its system. A Zephyr radiator fits just right and allows use of standard Ford hoses.

The Minor axle will not take the extra power though, and must be changed for something stronger and with taller gearing. Use of a Ford one makes it easy to get a propshaft shortened to fit.

Fiat twin-cam engine

Minor modifiers finally found the best of all worlds in Aurelio Lampredi's four-cylinder masterpiece. Used in a variety of capacities from 1300 to 2000cc in Fiats and Lancias from 1966, this alloy-headed engine is light, strong, free-revving and was used in a succession of cars that rusted away long before the engine gave out. This left a decent stock of donor material in breakers' yards.

Credit for the first installation of a Fiat twin-cam into a Minor goes to Alan Weight in the late 1970s. A few others followed, including, in 1983, Russ Smith. After carrying out a couple of such swaps and using a converted car on a daily basis, he got together with Unique Autocraft in Harlow to produce a complete kit for the conversion, consisting of engine mounts and rubbers, gearbox and new front crossmembers, two-into-one exhaust downpipe and clutch cable bracket. This was launched in June 1988. Over the next five years, and before the rights to the kit were bought by Minor Mania, around 90 were sold. Add in the 11 cars converted by the Beardmore brothers in Yorkshire, around 20 kits produced by other specialists and the many home conversions carried out, and it is a fair estimate that some 150 Minors have been converted to Fiat twin-cam power.

The benefits are great: the engines come with tough five-speed gearboxes, require little maintenance, produce plenty of power and do not upset the handling balance. A Minor fitted with a 2-litre twin-cam can be expected to reach 110mph and accelerate to 60mph in eight seconds; 28-30mpg is normal, too.

Datsun engines

Australia probably has the second-largest population of Minors in the world and, faced with a very different stock of donor vehicles, the Australians took a very different route for alternative engines. Thanks to a comprehensive kit produced by Kelly Products which contained all mounts, exhaust, hoses and accessories, there are now hundreds of Minors in Australia running Datsun engines in 1000, 1200 and 1400cc capacities. These conversions do not produce out-and-out road-burners, but they do represent a popular and reliable alternative for keeping Minors on the road in a country where A-series engine and gearbox parts are not so freely available.

The future

There is much speculation as to the next source of extra power once the supplies of Fiat and indeed Marina and Ital engines dry up. Options are limited by manufacturers' wholesale switch to front-wheel drive, and complicated by the burgeoning use of computers and electronics in modern cars. Backyard engineers tend to shy away from such technology at the moment, but the computer age is with us and general familiarity with modern electronics is growing all the time.

Fitting a transverse front-wheel drive unit to a Minor is certainly possible in theory, using a complete subframe-mounted engine/suspension unit, although track width would be a limiting factor in the narrow Minor. It would also completely change the Minor's character.

A more likely answer would lie in one of the engines that is still adapted for use in rear-drive cars by specialist manufacturers like Morgan and Caterham. Rover's K-series seems the most obvious choice, having a family connection and being both compact and light. Also in its favour, the aftermarket already produces carburettor conversions for these engines along with programmable electronic control units. There is also Ford's Zetec unit, which comes in 1600, 1800 and 2000cc capacities. Only time will tell.

Using a modern five-speed gearbox

Credit for the first adaptation of a five-speed gearbox to an A-series Minor engine goes to Kelly Products in Australia, who produced a

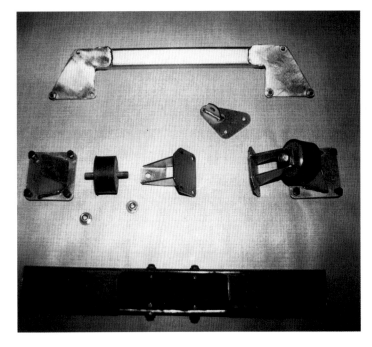

Unique Autocraft's Fiat twin-cam installation kit for a Minor shows, from the top: front crossmember, clutch cable bracket, engine mounts and gearbox crossmember.

bellhousing to attach a Toyota Celica gearbox in the 1980s. The idea then spread to America and finally to Britain where it was marketed by Rooster Racing. Interest has recently declined as suitable gearboxes have become scarce. In America, Bruce Wyman developed a similar idea using a Datsun B210 five-speed gearbox.

The baton has been picked up by several specialists like the Morris Minor Centre Birmingham and CS Autoclassics, who now offer five-speed conversions using the far more plentiful Ford Sierra gearbox. Relaxed high-speed cruising is the main advantage.

Uprating the brakes

As a standard Minor's brakes are barely adequate, tuned cars have always needed help in the stopping department. Servos have long been a popular addition, but the more useful fitting of larger front drums had to wait until the introduction of the Wolseley 1500 and Riley One-Point-Five. Both shared the Minor's front suspension assembly, and this made transferring their brakes to a Minor a bolt-on job. Both cars used 9in diameter drums (early Minors used 7in, later ones 8in), although the Riley's were also wider to match its more powerful engine.

The now-common disc brake conversions were a surprisingly long time coming. *Hot Car* magazine ran a feature on fitting Triumph Herald discs to a Minor in March 1978, but as this

The early (left) and later (right) Fiat five-speed gearboxes here show the amount that must be cut from their bellhousings to clear the Minor's steering rack. Experts prefer the early type, which needs less gearbox tunnel modification to fit the Minor and has a better shift quality.

required much complicated machining, including the fabrication of new stub axles, it was never destined to take off in a big way.

The first bolt-on kit was made by Kelly Products in Australia in the late 1970s utilising MG Midget parts, the key to which were specially machined caliper mounting brackets to fit the Minor uprights. This was soon followed by similar offerings from Morriservice in California and Spridgebits Ltd in Birmingham, who had such a kit for sale by 1982.

A complete Marina disc brake conversion kit.

The first Marina disc brake conversion was offered by Carsmiths of Norwich in early 1985. It used a combination of spacers and new outer bearings to adapt the Marina hubs to the Minor stub axles. The company advertised one version that used Marina wheels, and a more expensive one with exchange hubs converted back to Minor stud pattern. Both, however, substantially undercut the price of the Midget disc conversion, and with Marina parts more plentiful in breakers' yards the die was cast; nearly all Minor specialists now offer such a conversion kit.

Suspension modifications

The Morris Minor's torsion bar front suspension is excellent from a tuner's point of view. It is let down only by the cost-cutting fitment of leaf springs at the rear which allow axle tramp even on a standard-engined car. In the 1960s Allard offered anti-tramp bars to cure this weakness.

Improvements in the damping department arrived in the early 1970s when Spax launched front and rear telescopic damper kits to do the duty of the standard lever arms. These are still available and a popular fitment to any Minor today.

Also offered in the 1960s was a front anti-roll bar from V.W. Derrington, which in 1969 cost £5 5s 0d. Little else was done seriously until the late 1980s, however, when development of the Minor's handling really took off, with many specialists offering their

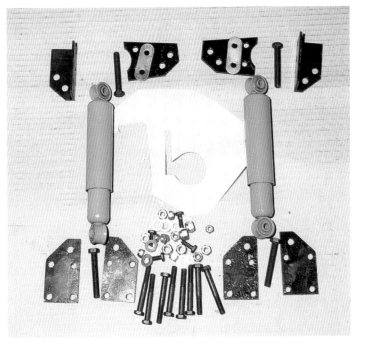

Spax telescopic damper conversions (far left) for the Minor have been fitted to hundreds of cars since the early 1970s. A typical front telescopic damper kit (near left) from another manufacturer is also shown.

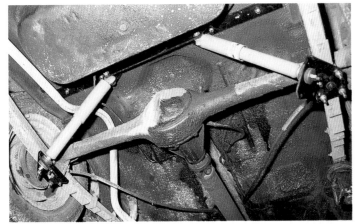

One version of the rear telescopic damper conversion has dampers canted inboard in a similar fashion to the Minor van. Others have the dampers inclined rearwards, parallel to the springs, or upright, turreted into the inner wings.

own solutions and making good use of modern materials.

Minor owners can now buy anything from uprated torsion bars down to nylon bushes to replace the suspension rubbers. There are many telescopic damper options, anti-roll bars, anti-tramp bars, negative camber front suspension eyebolts and even anti-bump-steer kits for lowered cars. CS Autoclassics have developed a new wishbone front suspension set-up during 1997 – still the quest goes on to modify the Minor.

All this means that a Minor's handling can be made more than a match for any power increase the car might be given – an important factor in the safety-conscious 1990s.

One of the many front anti-roll bars now available, this one is from Mr Grumpy's Morris Minors.

CUSTOM MINORS

Gary Ellis's convertible in shots that span two decades. In Hot Car for June 1969 (right), it was the first great custom Minor; several revamps later in Street Machine for May 1989 (below) it was still the greatest, combining a fuel-injected Rover V8 with the finest craftsmanship in its build.

The Morris Minor has been a solid cornerstone of the British customising scene since the late 1960s. Its popularity as a custom car has grown rather than diminished, and since 1979 it has been the third most featured model of car in *Street Machine*, the UK's top custom magazine.

Eclipsed only by the 'sit up and beg' Ford Popular and the prolific VW Beetle, the Minor was and still is a popular choice for first-time customisers. The Beetle did not really take off as a custom car until the mid-1980s, when the Cal-look trend blew in from America and struck a chord with young car enthusiasts. The Ford Popular proved better suited to the more experienced customisers, who were more inclined to build their vehicles to what magazines termed 'feature standard'. In consequence, custom Minors far outnumber other marques.

Up until 1969 few people modified Minors, and those who did were considered strange. Minis and Anglias were the thing, and the Minor's image was rather frumpy. Two things changed all that, however. The first was the growing availability of easy-to-fit 1275cc MG Midget power (see page 99), and the second was a car featured in the June 1969 issue of *Hot Car* – at the time Britain's

Alex Scott's 'Li'l Queenie' was an inspiration to many after a feature in Custom Car in May 1973. It was powered by a 2-litre Ford V4 and its many body modifications were enhanced by a fine example of 1970s excess, metalflake paint. Alex took the car to two big custom car shows and came home with eight trophies!

Radical front end concealing a 3.5-litre Rover V8 ensured plenty of attention for Chris Sandbach's convertible (left) which appeared on the cover of Custom Car in March 1980.

Bob Kember's classy MGB-powered two-door (above) was rather subtle and understated for 1978. But through the Leyland Damask Red paint screamed a clear and tempting message

from the pages of Hot Car: you too could have a car like this! Many heeded the call and, flared wings excepted, this was the look many custom Minors would emulate during the eighties.

Alan Weight's Minor was the first of many to be fitted with a Fiat twin-cam engine, sometime in the late 1970s. Originally a saloon, it was cut down into a roadster (no roof at all) in 1982 and fitted with a Wood & Pickett interior rescued from a Mini.

Badge engineering gone crazy? In 1982, Steve Riand grafted an Austin A40 Devon bonnet and grille onto his four-door Minor, and installed a supercharged 2.5-litre Daimler V8 engine beneath them.

only custom magazine – that instantly endowed the Minor with credibility. *Hot Car's* Paul Davies described Gary Ellis's convertible as 'the Ultimate Morris Minor', while the magazine's editor Tony Bostock went even further and crowned it 'Custom Car of the Past 12 Months'.

In bright orange with prototype Mosquito-like louvred bonnet and Emery alloy wheels under its flared arches when most customs of the day still used wide steel items, the car screamed for attention. A Shorrock-supercharged 1275cc engine made sure that when it got that attention it was no disappointment; acceleration from 0 to 60mph in well under 10 seconds and a top speed of well over 100mph were normally still the preserve of sports cars in 1969, not Morris Minors! Gary continued to develop the car at a rapid pace for several years. In 1970 it was probably the first custom car to be fitted with Ford's newly-launched 3-litre V6. Later he stored the Minor for several years while pursuing other projects, but came back to it in the 1980s.

The result was just as avant-garde as the 1969 incarnation. Twenty years on from that first feature, in May 1989, the car graced

the cover of *Street Machine's* 10th Birthday issue with the strapline 'Towards the next ten years'. Now powered by a fuel-injected 3.9-litre Rover V8, the convertible had received a roof chop, some of the most desirable American alloy wheels, and deep red paint over a bodyshell blessed with enough clever tricks to send custom Minor enthusiasts the world over rushing to the garage with fresh inspiration. Paul Jeffries concluded his article in *Street Machine* by re-crowning it 'the Ultimate Morris Minor', and no-one who has ever seen the car has disputed that claim.

In the intervening years changes in customising fashion have taken the Minor through a distinct evolution. This has been punctuated by particular milestone cars, many of them illustrated here. The greatest boost, however, came in 1974 with the film *American Graffiti*. Instantly, a generation wanted to go cruising the street, American-style, and the most plentiful car around which had the right look – the curved styling of an early post-war American machine – was the Morris Minor. Anyone could get one and many did. London's famous Chelsea Cruise, which started the following year and has been held on the last Saturday of every month ever

The spirit of 1950s America inspired the many body modifications to Nick Taylor's Ford V6-engined custom. Chopped roof, slanted B-pillars, peaked headlamps and flame paint were all the work of Southend's Richard King. Bonneville-style Moon Disc spun aluminium wheel covers soon became a popular low-budget choice.

since, was never without a sizeable contingent of Minors until the late 1990s when the Cruise became the domain of a new generation resplendent in hot hatches with pounding stereos.

Like so many other things in life, a custom car can be pretty accurately consigned to a particular era by elements of its make-up. A hot Minor of the early 1970s would typically have had a standard paint colour, perhaps with a vinyl roof, a B-series or Ford V4 engine, flared wheel arches, steel wheels and without doubt a black vinyl interior. Those steel wheels died a fairly quick and painless death around 1975. Though the British Wolfrace alloy wheels (initially spelt Woolferace) had been around for a couple of years, suddenly they were the thing to have on a Minor, and remained so for the next ten years. It may be a coincidence but 1975 also happened to see the debut of another inspiring milestone custom Minor: George Watt's wild Mustang V8-powered 'Astral Traveller', which confusingly was not a Traveller at all but a 1951 two-door saloon.

A couple of years later, the black vinyl started to be displaced by a velvety fabric called Dralon, preferably buttoned, and the thicker the foam it was stretched over the better. Up until the end

of the so-called Decade that Taste Forgot, custom car owners could also draw gasps of admiration by trimming the tops of dashboards and window surrounds in shaggy fake fur and running rows of tassels round the edge of the headlining. Paint finishes were just as drastic. Those who could afford professional custom paint jobs went for Metalflakes, Candies and even murals, while those who did their own work were more likely just to fog the edges of panels in a contrasting colour.

A new decade brought a complete change in attitude. The customising hobby had passed its anything-goes escapist fun period, and began to take itself seriously. This may have reflected a general culture change, or may just have been that those involved in the hobby were no longer teenagers and were merely growing up. It was also a time when more hardware became available from aftermarket suppliers, more radical modifications were experimented with, and much influence was being drawn from the America of the 1950s.

The rise of the Minor within the custom scene was greatly advanced by the Custom Minor Club. Formed in March 1981 by Nick Diss and Russ Smith (who later went on to edit *Street Machine*

Pete Levick's chopped two-door Minor wears one of the fibreglass Willys-style bonnets with a matching grille piece – a way of making your Minor different that really caught on after the showing in Britain of the TV film Hot Rod, which featured a 1941 Willys coupé as its star.

A testament to the bodyman's art, Lee McDouall's MG Midget-engined two-door has had every single panel on the car reworked in some way. Even the bulge that runs back into the door has been squared off, and that new grille was carved from aluminium to follow the lines of a grafted-on Austin Devon nose. Jaguar Mk2 bumpers, a roof chop and Triumph Herald sills explain only a small part of the whole picture.

With the look of a drag strip refugee, Pete Vorley's high-riding chopped two-door backed up its mean stance with a supercharged 3-litre Ford V6. This car was one of the first to appear with Centerline drag racing wheels on the front.

The Pro Street look (right) – basically a V8 engine and fat rear tyres under standard wings – swept the custom scene in the mid-1980s. Chris Nash built the first Pro Street Minor in 1985, using a Rover V8 and a narrowed Volvo axle on a home-built chassis.

Built in 1984, Mike Kason's clever little truck (below) wore a Willys nose – the first to be made as a one-piece replacement front end. But the most clever bit was the Mazda pick-up bed, shortened by 2¹/2 feet and narrowed by 6in to fit the Minor and carry the Honda trike.

A custom so good they built it twice! Richard King's Purple People Eater (centre left) was an icon to Minor customisers in the early 1980s. Sadly it was dismantled, but Simon Mower managed to rescue the pick-up bed and built a replica in 1990. Richard King was so pleased that he donated the Moon Discs to Purple People Eater II.

Robin Beardmore's pick-up (lower left) was stunning in more than just colour. Inventive in concept and immaculate in execution, it became Street Machine Feature Car of the Year in 1992. With a two-piece lift-off roof, Fiat twin-cam engine, the latest alloy wheels and super-smooth lines, it showed the way forward for the 1990s.

One of the most hard-used custom Minors, Russ Smith's four-door racked up over 80,000 miles in modified form. The car popularised Fiat twin-cam conversions, collected show trophies, ran regularly on drag strips and still provided everyday transport throughout the 1980s. It was timed at 7.55 seconds for the 0-60mph dash and could reach 110mph.

This is the ultimate expression of the Pro Street look combined with the subtlety of the mid-1990s. Nic Cook's chopped two-door Minor has power from a 5-litre Ford V8 and steamroller tyres. A Street Machine cover car in September 1994, it once again set new standards for those that will surely follow.

help set it up and produce the newsletter, and the Register is still active in the late 1990s, now run by Andi Kyle.

The first proper roof chops – that is, those which did not require the results to be hidden beneath a vinyl roof covering – were carried out by Richard King from Southend, although there is record of a convertible being chopped by Kris Brown in the mid-1970s. Richard King's first was for Nick Diss. A second, which was documented for a 'How To' feature in *Hot Car*, was commissioned by Tim Lane. The basic technique on a Minor was to cut three inches from each roof pillar, pull the roof forward to line up on the front posts, and then rework the rear window area to flow into the bodywork again.

Another body modification which became popular at this time was the so-called Willys front. This involved replacing the Minor's familiar face with a more pointed bonnet and matching grille piece which resembled that of the 1940-1941 American Willys Coupé, though it was originally designed with the intention of aping a 1940 Ford. Why someone should want to do this, apart from the customiser's natural desire to be different, is almost wholly explained by a cult TV film, *Hot Rod*, which starred just such a Willys Coupé.

The replacement front was actually first produced in 1975 by Kris Brown, Geoff Jago and Richard Park, and marketed as a Mako front, the first being fitted to Kris's chopped convertible. In the early days it was sold as a separate bonnet and add-on grille extension, but in 1982 Kris Brown, now with Unique Autocraft in Harlow, reworked it into a one-piece fibreglass replacement front end including the wings. This was at the request of a customer, Mike Kason, who wanted it for his red pick-up, which also featured a unique pick-up bed built to carry an off-road trike. Mike's pick-up was featured in the September 1984 issue of *Street Machine*. These fronts became very popular and the mould for making them still exists, now in the hands of Mighty Minor.

There was also a far greater choice of wheels available in the 1980s. At the expensive end of the market, these included lightweight Centerline aluminium wheels and Appliance chrome four-spokes. The latter's reputation quickly faded as they suffered badly if used on salty roads. As a budget option, many went for Moon Discs, the spun aluminium dished wheel covers made popular by speed record racers at Bonneville Salt Flats who used them as aerodynamic aids. Fitted to standard Minor rims, often in partnership with whitewall tyres, they gave a real 1950s feel. So too

and *Popular Classics* magazines), the club's membership quickly grew to three figures. Exchange of information through a monthly newsletter did much to educate and encourage people with their projects over the next three years, while the cultish style of the newsletter also developed something of a following outside Minor circles, thanks to reviews in the various custom magazines. The vacuum left by the disbanding of the club was filled in late 1987 by a Custom Register within the Morris Minor Owners Club. Committee Member Paul McLaughlin persuaded Russ Smith to did the flame paint jobs favoured by many. Dralon interiors continued for a while but lost their buttons. By the mid-1980s, they had almost completely given way to either pleated vinyl – a style referred to as 'tuck 'n' roll' – or the sort of cloths used in modern cars.

By this time another trend was sweeping the custom scene. This was the Pro Street look, derived from the Pro Stock class of drag racing. The basics were a powerful V8 engine and the fattest possible tyres that would fit under standard rear wings (flares were not allowed). This meant narrowing the rear axle and, for the Minor as for most other cars, a new purpose-built chassis and suspension. In effect all that was left of the original Minor was simply the bodyshell!

The first Pro Street Minor was built by Chris Nash, though it did not appear in a magazine (*Custom Car*) in this form until October 1988, by which time it had been sold to Jon Hill. Powered by a 3.5-litre Rover V8, it had a Volvo axle narrowed enough to fit 235/60x15 tyres under the back on wheels twice the width of standard Minor items.

Growing alongside Pro Street was a style which never got a name but was a lot more accessible and therefore more popular. Lowered suspension and smoothed-out bodywork were the key elements. Badges and trim would be removed or painted to match the body colour; some owners even went as far as flattening out the raised beltline along the side of the car. Under the bonnet, where the preferred power source was Fiat twin-cam (though Marina engines were also quite common), things were even smoother. There was a kind of unofficial competition to see how much could be removed from the engine bay and how flat the bulkhead and inner wings could be made. The ultimate expression of this was achieved by Robin Beardmore when he first showed his amazing pink pick-up in 1989.

Even old hands in the custom world stopped to take a good look at what had been created from a crash-damaged Post Office Telephones van by this talented 19-year-old. Apart from an engine bay that appeared to contain nothing but the engine itself and a throttle cable, the pick-up cab had a two-piece lift-off roof that stowed in the bed under a hard tonneau cover. There was a re-skinned smooth tailgate with a hand-formed curved valance beneath it; there were no door handles or badges and there were

many more clever tricks, all painted in the brightest pink you can imagine. It graced the November 1989 cover of *Street Machine*.

Even this multi-trophy-winning creation was not enough for the fertile Beardmore imagination. Three years later, he revamped it with a host of new tricks and a less controversial coating of blue-green Fiat paint. The bonnet was now hinged at the front, and the doors from the rear, suicide-style. The latter were fitted with smaller quarterlights to make room for larger window glass. The dashboard puzzled many by being completely blank, though in fact the gauges dropped down on a pod from behind when the engine was running. In this form the pick-up was again featured by *Street Machine*, in September 1992. Later, readers of the magazine voted it Feature Car of 1992, out of 49 candidates.

Late in the 1990s the trend seems almost to have turned full circle. Though loud and showy Minors are still being built, there is a general swing to the retro-look. Plain steel wheels are being used again, along with more sober colours and vinyl interiors. Whatever trend is in vogue, however, custom Minors look set to ring the changes and challenge the more innovative Minor enthusiasts well into the next millennium!

The role of the Minor in the custom scene was greatly enhanced by the Custom Minor Club and its cultish newsletter, which was widely praised.

ONE-OFFS AND SPECIALS

Views and opinions about the Morris Minor are as diverse as the variety of models produced. For all those who express a preference for seeing and preserving the car in its original form, there are just as many who prefer to extend the scope, design and performance of Alec Issigonis's original concept.

The extent to which these differing views have been reconciled is a moot point but the individual flair, commitment, effort and time channelled into the preservation and restoration of existing vehicles or the development of new ideas is an ongoing source of pleasure for Minor owners, enthusiasts and admirers alike. In keeping with other marques, the Morris Minor has appeared in many non-original guises, and this chapter reviews some of the more significant examples of the past 50 years.

Factory specials

A unique non-production Morris Minor still exists in the Heritage Motor Centre at Gaydon, Warwickshire. Built by the Body Development Department at Cowley, the Morris Minor Fire Engine was pressed into service with Morris Motors as a first-response vehicle in 1952. Being small and low, it could move quickly through factory congestion and arrive at the source of a fire well before a larger appliance.

As built, the fire engine was based on an early prototype Traveller chassis, and all the contemporary fittings including a side-valve engine were incorporated. Extensive modifications were made in 1963 to update the vehicle. A 1098cc engine and gearbox replaced the side-valve unit and original transmission, and even the fascia and the steering wheel of that year were added. In its present guise, the only items which betray the fire engine's true age are the Series MM style short bonnet and the split windscreen. This distinctive vehicle remained in service until 1974, when it was disposed of by British Leyland. Restored by the Historic Morris Fire Engine Club, it has been fully equipped with fire-fighting equipment and is now part of the permanent exhibition at Gaydon.

Most of the prototype and experimental Morris Minors were scrapped, but many are fondly remembered. Cars like the Mosquito exist only in photographs and in a rare scale model owned by Jack Daniels, who was Alec Issigonis's right-hand man on the design team. Jack has distinctive memories of another experimental car which he drove for years – a front-wheel drive, transverse-engined Morris Minor Saloon which he once described as the safest car he'd ever driven, especially in winter. It was a significant car too and, as Jack recalled, "I still regard it as an influential car which played a major role in preparing the way for the Mini Minor".

Nevertheless, two prototypes did survive, although their reclassification as production vehicles has left an intriguing tale of confusion. The first of these was registered 122 AJO, and was a Morris 1000 convertible which survived until at least 1985. Built on July 23rd, 1956 with the experimental chassis number EX307 (later changed to EX311), this vehicle was first registered by Morris Motors on September 17th, 1956. It was fitted with engine number APJM/H/4541, was painted turquoise and had grey interior trim.

After four years with Morris Motors, the car was sold in 1960 to Graham Wing in Oxford. At this point the engine was changed and the chassis number DO/1076/476 allocated. Eighteen years later, however, the DVLC insisted that it should carry a hybrid number on its V5 registration document, and the car became DO/1076/EX311. This experimental number was then scratched on the identification plate between DO/1076 and 476. When asked if this prototype had any unusual features, former owner Graham Loder recalled that it had special jacking points at the front and that the speedometer had a trip fitted to it. Apart from that it was a standard Morris 1000 convertible – but a unique one for all that.

Another prototype of sorts survives and has been fully restored by members of the Morris Minor Owners Club in the Dorset area. In late November 1960, a two-door saloon with chassis number 881386 was taken out of normal production to be turned into the prototype Morris Minor Million. The idea was to celebrate the historic landmark of one million Morris Minors of all types being produced. This was to be the one and only special edition Morris Minor, and 349 replicas of this prototype were made between December 13th and 22nd. The prototype, however, had white vinyl seat facings whereas the 349 replicas had white leather.

Other special features of the limited-edition Minor Million included black piping on the seats, black carpets, special chrome badges and wheel rim embellishers. However, the most distinctive feature was the lilac paint colour which was adopted instead of the planned silver, apparently because of technical difficulties at ICI who were unable to produce the favoured silver metallic paint.

Apart from its lilac paintwork and status as a prototype, what makes Minor number 881386 stand apart from other Morris Minors is the fact that it was issued with two chassis numbers. The car was renumbered into the special sequence reserved for Minor Millions and acquired the new number 1000330, which duly appeared on the chassis identification plate. However, the original chassis number 881386 still appears on the bulkhead of the vehicle to confirm its identification as the prototype car. Factory records show that chassis number 881386 was re-issued to a Yukon Grey four-door saloon built on December 16th, 1960. If this car survives, then technically two Morris Minors exist with the same chassis number!

Travellers

The factory produced a few variants of the versatile Traveller for export. The Morris 1000 Combi was marketed in Denmark and Norway and differed from standard models in that its rear windows were replaced by steel panels, which in effect made it a van with rear seats. The reason for this odd configuration was financial, blanked-off rear side windows meriting a tax concession which saved 30% on the cost of the vehicle.

There were also some coachbuilt versions of the Traveller. One of the most striking was the Crossley Berkshireman which was produced by Geoffrey Crossley Industries Limited of Croft Road, Wallingford, Berkshire. Built on a Morris Minor $^1/_4$-ton chassis, it featured walnut-veneered rear panels in a stout framework of fine seasoned ash. This framework differed significantly from the standard factory version and the rear doors were of a completely different design. A separate lower rear panel housed the rear lights and the number plate. Additional features included a detachable weatherproof roof panel. Aimed at a specific market, this unique vehicle sold for £766 15s 0d and was advertised as being suited for 'rough country usage'.

Individual ventures provided interesting variations on the Traveller's basic design. Special adaptations of the rear door arrangement were popular, and many had a one-piece rear window incorporated into a hinged ash frame which opened upwards. A similar one-piece ash-framed panel pulled down to provide a tailgate. The chief advantages of this design were improved rearward visibility and better accessibility to the rear luggage compartment.

One of the most adventurous individual Traveller projects was undertaken in 1957, and was constructed by a qualified engineer using proper BMC blueprints. A pick-up cab and chassis provided the starting point for a novel design of a Traveller with three

This unique fire engine was once owned by Morris Motors and now resides at the Heritage Motor Centre in Gaydon, Warwickshire.

Designed for 'rough country usage', the Berkshireman estate conversion by Geoffrey Crossley Industries was based on a Minor quarter-ton light commercial chassis.

With metal panels instead of glass in the rear, the Traveller-based Minor 1000 Combi was designed to save Danish buyers a worthwhile amount in tax.

This artist's impression of the Australian Sports 80 illustrates to good effect the distinctive colour scheme and the decorative spare wheel housing. At £866 in Australian money, its classy looks and increased performance (courtesy of a twin-carburettor conversion) made it an attractive proposition.

owner, he adapted it so that it could be used for sleeping two people in comfort – a conversion which did not commend itself to the factory but one which Reg still regards as sensible and practical.

Convertibles

Sir Alec Issigonis always held true to his original concept of the Minor, and lamented the fact that American lighting regulations forced a radical change to the front-end styling of the Series MM. So quite what he would have made of the adaptions made to the Series MM Tourer by the Swiss company J.H. Keller is open to conjecture. This Zürich company, formerly known as Sports Car AG, operated as a Morris and Nuffield agent and offered a special conversion for the MM Tourer. Billed as the Schweizer Cabriolet Deluxe, it featured four wind-down windows and a specially designed hood which was fully retractable, giving the overall impression of a totally open car. An easy-to-fit tonneau cover was also included in the specification.

Another Swiss open conversion was featured in *The Motor* in 1951. In this case, the whole of the roof was removed, along with the front side window frames, to leave the car totally open from the front quarter-lights rearward. Transformation into a saloon could be achieved with some effort by fitting the standard roof, secured coupé-fashion with two clamps on the windscreen and a single-point bolt fixing at the rear, along with the specially adapted original front frames.

In Australia, the Minor was well received, but before long it was being given special treatment to improve its appearance and its speed. New South Wales BMC distributor Peter Lloyd Ltd offered the Morris Minor Sports 80 in Convertible or Saloon versions at a price of £866 including sales tax. Dubbed the most exciting sports

opening doors, two of which were on the passenger side. In addition, a new style of rear door arrangement which had a lot to commend it was included. The overall length of the car was increased by some eighteen inches and there was an increase in weight too.

Additional features included a specially designed sunroof and a redesigned interior with many unique features, including a split rear seat. Special locating pins were incorporated so that the seats could be folded to turn the the rear of the car into a sleeping area, and many other areas of the car used non-standard items. These included interior trim coverings, rear tailgate hinges, spare wheel compartment and Hillman Minx-derived rear light units.

No review of Travellers would be complete without reference to Reg Job, the draughtsman on Issigonis's original Minor design team. Reg owns a Limeflower Morris 1000 Traveller and, like the previous

convertible on the road, the Sports 80 certainly cut a dash with its unusual paint scheme and improved performance. Its specially tuned engine with twin carburettors, sports coil and special sports exhaust system improved acceleration and produced a top speed of 80mph. Another distinctive feature was the detachable continental-style spare wheel housing, resplendent with its Morris Sports 80 logo. This was a purely decorative feature, however, as the spare wheel was not actually mounted on the boot! Nevertheless it was claimed that the Sports 80 offered an extra large boot of twice the normal capacity.

Fast cars

The Sprite Morris 1000

Among the many cars which motoring personality Rivers Fletcher owned and raced, one stands apart from the rest. Affectionately known as the Sprite Minor 1000, for reasons which will become obvious, the car was purchased as an economy measure in the mid-1950s when Britain was severely hit by the Suez fuel crisis. Rivers, more used to what he terms 'thirsty' Jaguars, acquired a new 948cc Morris 1000 two-door saloon, a car which he grew to love so much that he decided to modify it, with the assistance of his close friend Graham Hill.

Graham, who went on to become a two-times Formula 1 World Champion, worked for John Sprinzel at the time and it was he who carried out the engine work. A complete Austin-Healey Sprite unit was used, with a Speedwell conversion. Power output was considerably increased and there followed other modifications which included bigger and stronger dampers.

The car was resprayed in Rivers Fletcher's trademark blue. New carpets, more comfortable seats, revised instrumentation, a racing steering wheel and a full-length sun roof all followed, but the most distinctive feature was the addition of a Sprite grille in place of the standard Minor item. Complemented by twin spotlights and period wheel trims, this had the effect of identifying ONT 777 as something special.

Rivers used the car as everyday transport for the duration of the Suez crisis and then returned to his more favoured Jaguars. However, the Sprite Minor remained in the family and was used by Rivers' wife, Penny, both as a shopping car and in competition. The car was a family favourite and was eventually used by the couple's

The Schweizer cabriolet de luxe was offered for sale by the Zürich-based Nuffield distributor J.H. Keller, and featured a fully retractable hood.

Graham Hill worked on this 'Sprite Minor', which was owned by motor racing ace Rivers Fletcher. Purchased during the Suez crisis in 1957, it was painted in Rivers' famous blue and had a limited competition history.

son, Peter, when he went on his honeymoon to France. Regrettably, it seems that the car was eventually scrapped.

The Miller Minor

For a roadgoing Morris Minor, 105mph is some achievement, but a very special Minor achieved just that and in the process saw off highly-tuned Mini Cooper Ss and a lot of other contemporary 'hot' cars. The car was built by David Miller of Border Garage, West Wenlow, in Hampshire and was tested by *Motor* magazine in 1973. With 110bhp and an impressive 0-60mph time of 8.4 seconds, this brown 1958 convertible Minor certainly had some extra oomph!

Power was derived from a 1293cc engine built from a Mini Cooper S block, a 1275cc Sprite crank, and a BLMC 1300 GT cylinder head with larger inlet valves. A Sprite inlet manifold with

This high-roof van was originally owned by Curry's, the high street electrical retailers, and was specially designed to carry the then-new upright fridge-freezers.

You've always a bedroom

on the MORRIS DORMOBILE Junior

BRITISH PATENT No. 703225 (Overseas Patents Pending)

No worries about where to sleep on holidays or weekend trips when you've this remarkable adaptable Dormobile. The seating can be arranged in seconds to form two full-sized beds! And it takes a jiffy to rearrange to carry four people for pleasure drives or to convert into a flat-floor delivery and collection van. On the same chassis as the economical ¼-ton Morris it is well worth investigating now.

£610·5·10 inc. P.T.

There is also a larger Morris Dormobile—a conversion of the ½-ton Morris Van.

Full details of either model from Nuffield dealers or the designer.

Martin Walter *Ltd*

'UTILECON' Registered DESIGNERS

UTILECON WORKS

FOLKESTONE **ENGLAND**

Phone: FOLKESTONE 51844 Established 1773

The versatility of the light commercial vehicle chassis is shown to good effect by this well-executed caravanette. Made by Jim Lambert, it is a compact and fully-equipped two-berth unit.

Martin Walter of Folkestone carried out a number of approved conversions on Morris commercial vehicles. This effective rear seat conversion added further to the versatility of the popular commercial variants of the Minor.

American Minor specialist Bruce Wyman of Morris Service in California built this special articulated Minor. A standard Minor could be accommodated on the semi-trailer.

Used by Minor Mania, a London specialist, this six-wheeler breakdown recovery truck certainly proved its worth; the wheels on the extra axle were undriven. This Manchester-based ice-cream van with a specially-adapted high top was a popular visitor with adults and children alike.

twin H4 SU carburettors, a Miller-modified 544 cam and a Maxiflow manifold with a straight-through exhaust completed a very potent package. Suspension modifications included the fitting of what were described as 'cunningly angled' Koni shock absorbers to the rear, and stopping power was improved by the fitting of Riley One-Point-Five discs on the front, along with a servo.

Variously described as the Mighty Minor and the Miller Minor, JEP 261 was a well-sorted machine. *Motor* magazine's Gordon Bruce described it as the closest thing he'd come across to being the "ultimate wolf in sheep's clothing". He was seriously impressed with the car but did wonder if the convertible top had been designed to cope with 105mph!

Commercials

The light commercial vehicles lent themselves much more readily to special conversions, not least because of their separate chassis.

When new, the commercials were available in a variety of stages of build. Complete vans and pick-ups ready painted in standard colours were supplied through the dealer network in the normal way, but chassis-cab versions could be purchased with an enclosed cab or without the cab back, thus enabling the customer to have a design of his own choice fitted by a coachbuilder. This degree of flexibility has allowed for a great variety of vehicles to be produced, and a selection is pictured here.

The post-production Minor

The craving to have a new or as-new example of something which is no longer available is an understandable one, and without it the classic car restoration hobby would be very much the poorer. However, the quest for a 'new' Minor has taken some individuals into new realms of research as they set about acquiring the thousands of components which go to make up a complete car.

Unavailability of original rear panels for the van and pick-up bodies has given rise to a number of home-made wooden flat-bed conversions. The specially lengthened back on this example (near right) was still based on the standard LCV chassis. The Australian Morris Minor Centre used a Morris 1000 commercial (far right) or 'ute' in the local vernacular, as the basis of a very neat breakdown truck.

One of the first to undertake this task was Mr Law (Senior) from Swindon, Wiltshire, who in 1974 decided to order a new Morris Minor using the good offices of Dutton Forshaw of Swindon who agreed to co-ordinate the research process and assemble the vehicle. Parts were sourced from the extensive British Leyland dealership network, and in the end the only difficulty was finding an interior to original specification. This was overcome by

commissioning a hand-made one. The car was eventually finished in 1975 and registered GHR 800N, and cost a staggering £3625.04, only five years after factory-produced saloons had been selling for £770. For that price, Mr Law could have bought himself a 3-litre Ford Granada and pocketed a few hundred pounds in change – but he chose to have an obsolete Minor instead.

A similar undertaking involving the creation of a 'new'

Dutton Forshaw in Swindon were commissioned to find all the parts to build a new Morris Minor in 1974. The final cost of the car was £3625. It was later used in a local charity event.

Traveller was undertaken by Jim Steel several years later. In this case, the parts were acquired by Appleyards of Leeds, although the assembly process was undertaken at home. An unavoidable break of five years in the car's construction complicated the undertaking, but eventually the job was finished. The car was registered with one of the Q-prefix numbers given to kit cars and vehicles of indeterminate age.

Of course, new and unregistered Morris Minors still exist as well! A number of bodyshells complete with all panels and mechanical components have come to light in various technical colleges, where they have been used for educational purposes by students and apprentices. A new and unregistered van, still in factory primer and with just 36 miles on the clock, resides in Derbyshire, while in Ireland two CKD saloons assembled by Brittain's remain unregistered. The better-known of these is now owned by Paul Hanley from Dublin, who has obtained special dispensation to use it for charitable events and displays. Since it was assembled in 1975 following the liquidation of Brittain's, it has covered 2000 miles. The second Irish car came to light in 1996, having been bought and then stored for 25 years!

Post-factory development cars

The Minor's enduring appeal and its almost legendary longevity have persuaded specialists to undertake development work which will ensure its viability in the long term. Most individuals or companies undertaking work in this sphere have tried to retain the car's essential character while at the same time updating its mechanical components and internal specification.

Prominent in this field is Charles Ware from the Morris Minor Centre who in 1985 announced what he rather incongruously named a Series III Minor. This featured a 1275cc A-Series engine, a four-speed gearbox from the Sprite and Midget range of sports cars, and an Ital rear axle along with Ital disc brakes on the front and drums on the rear. With a vastly improved interior based on the Metro's and featuring fully-adjustable reclining front seats, the car has a more modern image and its performance for today's motoring appreciably improved. Certainly the Ware development car – a white Traveller registered WAH 793H – received rave reviews when tested by *Autocar* magazine.

Chris Street of CS Autoclassics has continuously been offering uprating packages for suspension and gearboxes, and his

Charles Ware, proprietor of the Morris Minor Centre at Bath, marketed a modernised version of the Minor which incorporated uprated suspension, a 1275cc A-series engine, and a revised interior derived from that found in the Austin Metro.

Chris Street of CS Autoclassics uses this Traveller as a development car. 'Merlin' has been used to test a variety of five-speed gearboxes and suspension modifications designed to make the Minor more serviceable as an everyday car in the 1990s.

development car known as Merlin has featured prominently in the press during the 1990s. He also developed a unique Morris Minor Cabrio in 1993, in association with owner Amanda Hazlett.

Amanda's considerable experience in working with Morris Minors, coupled with the insight into automotive engineering gained from her day job with Nissan, led her to contemplate designing a Minor for the 1990s. The Cabrio featured all of Chris Street's latest braking and suspension modifications, while power came from a 1275cc Marina engine driving through a Nissan (Datsun) five-speed gearbox. The interior, lavishly finished in Cobra Leatherette and Dralon, was a joy to behold. Much of the development work, however, had concentrated on creating a strengthened bodyshell, and the Cabrio featured side impact bars built into the sill area, a substantial cross beam and an integral roll cage. There was also a three-position convertible top, which gave the option of a 'Targa' mode in addition to the usual fully up and

This striking Morris Minor Cabrio with three-position convertible top was built for Amanda Hazlett in 1993. It has so far remained unique.

fully down positions. Although initial enthusiasm was high and the prospects for the order book were promising, the potential of the Cabrio has not yet been realised and for the moment Amanda's £15,000 Cabrio remains a one-off prototype.

Kit cars

After Minor production had stopped, many owners were faced with the prospect of expensive structural restorations on examples which had sound mechanical components capable of providing further useful service. To such people, the possibility of building the sound components into a Minor-based kit car had a certain appeal.

This Kilo kit car is one of only a dozen known to have been made between 1983 and 1986. It used Morris 1000 running gear on an all-steel chassis clothed in GRP bodywork.

Two options were available in the mid-1980s. The first was the Kilo Sports, a kit car produced by David Stiff of the 1000 Workshop based in Bodmin, Cornwall. The Kilo used all the main running gear components of the 1098cc Minor. However, because the engine was placed behind the steering rack, a lengthened steering column was used along with a shortened propshaft. This low-slung two-seater was built on a steel chassis and had a fibreglass body with one-piece, full-length wings and short running boards. At least 12 Kilos are thought to have been built.

The second Minor-based kit car was the Sonnet, again derived from the 1098cc Morris. It was offered for sale at £599 plus VAT in 1985 by Oldham and Crowther, a Peterborough-based Morris Minor specialist renowned for an innovative one-piece floor pan which nevertheless had limited success. The same can be said of the Sonnet which in truth was more of a concept car. It was described as having a pressed steel body and chassis with crumple zones for crash safety. Made with single-piece front and rear GRP mouldings, it had some similarities with the Kilo in that an exchange steering column and propshaft were part of the package, which also included a brake, clutch and throttle assembly and a rollover bar.

Bizarre and unusual

Some people delight in creating bizarre and unusual cars, and the Morris Minor has not escaped their attentions. If there were to be a prize for the most bizarre or unusual creations, however, it would probably go to one of four contenders.

The first one is a specially fabricated motorised 'Lobster' which was commissioned by Central TV in 1987 for a children's programme starring a character called Professor Lobster, who was an academic with a particular interest in architecture. Based on a Morris Minor saloon, the Lobster has a GRP tail grafted onto its boot lid and a pair of fully operational claws mounted on its doors. These claws were designed, produced and fitted in just two weeks by the Anglo-American Auto Service in Nottingham, and guarantee

limited funds, it came complete with a large sunroof and black side windows and was actually driveable. Interestingly, a one metre long clay model was made first, and from this a glass-fibre mould was taken. Model maker Richard Taylor then installed a radio control mechanism which enabled the glass-fibre model to be used for certain scenes.

Just as unusual – and technically fascinating – was a Minor pick-up used as a platform for experimenting with steam as a motive power. The paraffin fuelled boiler sat on the load deck with the steel cab back separating it from the driver and passenger. The engine was a four-cylinder double-acting unit which utilised the existing A-series engine from the top of the old block downwards. A complete new cylinder block with valve chest was constructed on top of the old block, which then used the existing pistons and bores as cross-heads to guide the new piston rods. Original transmission and running gear was unchanged.

Two became one! This 'stretch limo' was made in New Zealand out of two Minors, and starred in the film Meet the Feebles.

Finally the last word in unusual Minors has to go to Paul Smith. For reasons best known to himself, Paul joined the front ends of two Morris Minors together to create a unique street-legal car, which gives the impression that it is coming and going at the same time – or perhaps neither. The car has two facia panels and two steering wheels, but fortunately only one set of controls is operational!

Steam-powered Minor pick-up, seen during lengthy (and alarming looking!) start procedure, uses paraffin to heat the boiler and a modified A-series engine as motive power.

that the Lobster will turn heads wherever it goes. When filming ended, the Lobster was bought by Henric, the company which manufactures Morris Minor body panels. It is now used for charitable events and promotional work and is seen regularly at local shows and fêtes.

The second contender also comes from the film industry, and is a Morris Minor stretched limousine which was created in New Zealand. BLETCH 1 starred in Peter Jackson's *Meet the Feebles*, New Zealand's first major puppet feature film. Made from two cars, it was stretched by 1.5 metres. Although built as a prop and with

A firm favourite with children and an attention-grabber wherever it goes is the Lobstermobile. Created for a children's programme featuring Professor Lobster, it was subsequently bought by Minor specialists Henric, who use it for publicity purposes.

MINOR MISCELLANY

Morris Minors have often featured in the BBC children's programme Blue Peter over the years. Here, presenter Peter Duncan is seen with Roger Horton's Series MM Tourer in the TV studio in London.

Actor Windsor Davies starred in It Ain't Half Hot, Mum and in several other TV shows. He was pictured here with a convertible Minor on location for Never the Twain in 1992.

The 1993 film, Shadowlands, starred Sir Anthony Hopkins and this restored 1950 Series MM saloon. They are seen together in the Wye Valley during a break from filming.

When actress Prunella Scales appeared in the TV sitcom Searching in 1995, the Morris 1000 Traveller she drove brought back memories of Minor ownership in real life.

Havoline's easy to pour oil. It's almost foolproof.

Havoline 15w-40 oil. **TEXACO**

Michael Crawford in characteristic pose as Frank Spencer, star of Some Mothers Do Have 'Em in a contemporary advert for Havoline motor oil. The car still exists, in the hands of an enthusiastic owner.

A veritable plague of Morris Minors (near right) in the 1997 feature film, The Borrowers. In this film a uniquely equipped Minor van (far right) is the main mode of transport for the Pest Exterminator, played by Mark Williams.

A wide range of Morris Minor models has been available over the years, and this picture shows a number of the most notable.

1 Victory
2 Victory
3 Victory
4 Revell
5 Revell
6 Minic
7 Pathfinder
8 Spot-On
9 Matchbox
10 Corgi

Two detailed Morris Minor scenes featuring a Traveller ('A day in the country', price £275) and a Pick-up ('To the Tup Sale', price £210).

The Spot-On Morris Minor 1000 came in the range's regular 1/42nd scale and is now highly prized by collectors. Produced in Northern Ireland, the model came in blue or red.

Victory Industries produced a wonderful battery-powered two-door Morris Minor saloon model and – just like the real thing – brochures were produced to promote it. Front covers are seen for high-headlamp Series MM and Series II versions, and scales were respectively quoted at 1/18th and 1/16th. Inside the earlier brochure is a fascinating spread of factory scenes. These plastic models had die-cast detachable wheels, press-on wheel discs, Dunlop tyres and a steering mechanism based on the Ackerman principle. They could be had in a range of colours, including gold.

Making the model MORRIS MINOR

THE WORLD'S SUPREME MODEL CAR

MODELLED BY VICTORY INDUSTRIES (SURREY) LIMITED

IN COLLABORATION WITH THE NUFFIELD ORGANIZATION

THE MORRIS Minor

OFFICIAL SCALE REPLICA MODELLED BY VICTORY INDUSTRIES (SURREY) LTD.

IN COLLABORATION WITH THE NUFFIELD ORGANIZATION

This scratch-built radio-controlled replica model was made to 1/8th scale. It is constructed of balsa wood on an aluminium chassis.

Jimco's motorised miniature Minor has a glass-reinforced plastic body and provides a great deal of pleasure for its young drivers.

The 'Minor Junior' is billed as a high-quality, sleek and elegant pedal car designed for discerning drivers

between the ages of four and eleven. It is marketed by the Morris Minor Centre (Bath) Ltd.

This teapot with a difference is part of the 1997 range of products from The Teapottery in Keswick.

TOWARDS THE NEXT 50 YEARS

Many of the characteristics which attracted original owners to purchase their Morris Minors still commend themselves to new generations of owner drivers today. The wide range of models, each one with its distinctive styling and distinguished history, continues to attract both enthusiastic collectors and committed motorists, and all of them continue to perpetuate the Morris Minor legend.

A major factor which influences interest in the Morris Minor and its continued use is the wide network of UK-based spares specialists. Most components are available as remanufactured items and almost all mechanical components are capable of refurbishment, and in consequence the Morris Minor remains a fully practical means of everyday transport. The significance of body parts availability and the increased supply of repair panels cannot be underestimated. Although the prospect of complete new Morris Minor bodyshells remains a forlorn hope at present, the establishment of a Sri Lankan base for the production of hand-crafted panels has further supplemented the prolific range of British products which have sustained countless restorations and facilitated millions of essential repairs.

Renewed interest in the versatile range of light commercial vehicles has prompted a major rethink in recent years. The non-availability of replacement original metal panels for both the van and pick-up has spurred on the search for viable alternatives. In earlier times, the most practical option was to dispense with the original panels and fit a fabricated flat-bed back, but this has been superseded in the late 1990s by the production of glass-fibre panels.

These use the original internal metal frame and support brackets to enable the use of metal doors or a tailgate. With a new chassis also available, it is possible to buy a 'new' van once again, although the £7500 price tag (1997) appears in sharp contrast to the £455 asked for the genuine article in 1969. But then what other light van or pick-up with real character can be bought today for that sort of money?

A glass-fibre alternative known as the 'Traveller's Van' is also being promoted as a means of rejuvenating tired Travellers, and provides a rear moulding to replace all the panel work behind the cab. Only time will tell if radical alternatives like this have a place in the future in any significant numbers.

The adaptability of the Morris Minor has served it well in the past, and continues to play a major role in creating and retaining interest in the vehicles. Whether in Australia, Scandinavia, Britain or continental Europe, locally-sourced non-standard modern power units look set to be used in the future and will undoubtedly ensure that a significant percentage of vehicles which might otherwise be scrapped will enjoy a new lease of life.. The trend towards fitting more modern engines may become even more popular as environmental issues assume greater significance for motorists worldwide and, in Europe at least, the availability of leaded fuel seems set to be severely curtailed by the year 2000. Yet many Minors will certainly continue to run with their original engines, and many owners have already adopted the 'lead-free' cylinder head conversions which are readily available as exchange units. All these factors seem certain to prolong the debate among Minor owners about the benefits of original and modified cars!

GRP van and pick-up bodies are now available from British specialist Henric, and should ensure the long-term survival of many Light Commercial variants of the Minor.